D1739318

HYPER-PERFORMANCE

HYPER-PERFORMANCE

The A.I.M. Strategy for Releasing Your Business Potential

Errol R. Korn

George J. Pratt

with

Peter T. Lambrou

JOHN WILEY & SONS

New York • Chichester • Brisbane • Toronto • Singapore

This publication is designed to provide accurate and
authoritative information in regard to the subject
matter covered. It is sold with the understanding that
the publisher is not engaged in rendering legal, accounting,
or other professional service. If legal advice or other
expert assistance is required, the services of a competent
professional person should be sought. *From a Declaration
of Principles jointly adopted by a Committee of the
American Bar Association and a Committee of Publishers.*

Library of Congress Cataloging-in-Publication Data:

Korn, Errol R.
  Hyper-performance.

  Bibliography: p.
  1. Success in business. 2. Workaholics. I. Pratt,
George J. II. Lambrou, Peter T. III. Title.

HF5386.K775 1987   650.1   86-33984
ISBN 0-471-85344-5

Printed in the United States of America

10 9 8 7 6 5 4 3 2 1

Preface

In our work with thousands of clients and patients, we have observed some fascinating consistencies and some surprising corollaries. We have isolated some of those specific findings and matched them to new research, to studies, and to some of the classic observations and assumptions that are prevalent in both the popular press and in many professional circles.

In addition to the growing concern that stress is an insidious factor in causing many illnesses, stress related to work affects more than 80 percent of the working population. The cost to American business of this pervasive stress is enormous in terms of lost productivity, health benefits paid, lost innovation, future development, and additional resources diverted to counteract stress in the workplace.

However, those individuals who can cope with excessive stress counterbalance its harmful characteristics. They function in the same healthy way in which people not under excessive stress react. For example, in a University of Chicago study of executives of a local utility, only 20 percent of those under excessive stress became ill. The healthy majority of those stressed executives shared these three characteristics with individuals not experiencing excessive stress: (1) control, (2) commitment, and (3) the anticipation and perception of changes as exciting challenges.

Our intention is to provide a working plan to convert destructive stress into productive energy, by directing you or someone you are concerned about in utilizing the natural tendencies of the unconscious computer toward what we call hyper-performance. We have provided more than just a description of a theory, or anecdotal results. We offer a proven formula for effecting the positive changes and trait enhancements.

The techniques we describe as the A.I.M. Superskills have been used with professional and international athletes for over two decades. The Soviets and East Germans were pioneers in using mental rehearsal and mental workouts to achieve optimal performance. Western countries have been slow to apply these mental tactics. Notable exceptions, such as Jack Nicklaus, Ken Norton, Chris Evert-Lloyd, and Bill Russell, among other celebrated sports personalities, have openly professed that relaxation and imagery skills help them achieve their personal best.

Barbara Kolany did a 1978 study on basketball players at Hunter College, and found that mental rehearsal increased performance by 15 percent. We have found that the same techniques that have helped athletes perform better can be applied in the workplace to help business people become high-level achievers.

Our objective is to describe the 10 major characteristics of these optimal performers in the workplace, and present methods of change that we have observed and utilized that enhance those characteristics. The intention of this book is to help executives at many levels identify potential hyper-performers (also called new workaholics) and take steps toward hiring them when necessary, retaining them when possible, and helping all employees reach even higher levels of performance and achievement.

This is not easy, but it is phenomenally helpful in achieving corporate and individual success. Each of the authors is a self-avowed new workaholic. We take pride in the accomplishments we've attained thus far, and we recognize the potential to accomplish even more. If you are a CEO or president of an entrepreneurial firm, you may notice that you possess many of the optimal performance characteristics outlined in this book, and are well aware of traits you can improve. This book provides a sophisticated and long-lasting approach to enhancing those traits, with methods of helping subordinates reach higher levels of performance for the company and themselves.

We regularly conduct in-service workshops to show corporations the inner dynamics of new workaholic employees and how to maintain and even foster such traits. New workaholics are productive, happy, and healthy individuals: they enjoy work as a primary endeavor in life, and are high-level achievers who have harnessed the damaging effects of excessive stress while using their imagination to move closer and more swiftly toward their objectives.

Since less than 10 percent of the available workforce are hyper-performers or new workaholics, and about the same percentage are content, moderately productive, useful employees who are necessary to most organizations, the bulk of the workforce is made up of varying degrees of stressed-out people (SOPs).

This group of individuals ranges from downright poor employees seldom worth keeping on the payroll to fairly good workers who may even have flashes of brilliance. We describe these personality types to aid employers in recognizing and helping potential new workaholics achieve their goals and to help such individuals identify themselves and implement strategies to move themselves toward becoming hyper-performers.

The high value of the new workaholic to an organization may be self-evident to some people and may even be misconstrued to have little value by others. Here is what a new workaholic is capable of: innovation, sustained high levels of performance, a driving force that becomes a role model for other individuals motivated to achieve similar levels of accomplishment, and a highly productive component contributing to the overall profitability of the organization. That is also the very least that such hyper-performers expect of themselves.

ERROL R. KORN
GEORGE J. PRATT

Chula Vista, California
January 1987

Acknowledgments

We wish to thank the following individuals who have provided encouragement, support, and have assisted us in developing this book: Darren Korn, Joseph Korn, Meredith Korn, Mildred Korn, Nancy Korn, David Pratt, George Pratt, Sr., Sally Pratt, Whitney Pratt, Lyn Binkowski, Mary Ann Creel, Susan Freeman, Pete Johnson, Marilyn Lauer, Todd Morgan, our editor Mike Hamilton, Kirk Bomont, Kathy Astor and the entire production staff at John Wiley, and our collaborator, Peter Lambrou.

Contents

1

Portrait of a Hyper-Performer

*H*e is an enthusiastic and in-
tense individual who becomes absorbed in a project to a degree that astonishes his employees and colleagues. If there
were such a thing as a typical day he would be in the office by
6:30 A.M., scan the reports from the previous day, read several industry periodicals, then write memos to his executives.
By 9 o'clock in the morning he would preside over the first
meeting of the day.

By lunchtime he has engaged in four overseas phone conversations and 12 domestic calls and has had three personal
meetings with his various executives. He has lunch with the
head of his firm's advertising agency to strategize an upcoming campaign but at 3 P.M. he declines a hastily called meeting
by the CEO and leaves work to take his daughters out, something he'd promised them for weeks.

When he returns home he has dinner with his family, then
sequesters himself in his study to prepare for an important
meeting the next day in the nation's capital. He retires early,
knowing that he will be away from home for two days on
business.

The person whose day we've just described is Lee Iacocca,
during his post-Mustang years at Ford Motor Company.
Through this glimpse, and if you've read his biography or
autobiography, you will realize that he has blended his intense business life with a full family life, unlike the stereo-
typical workaholic of the past.

The Hyper-Performer — A New Workaholic

We have identified a new type of workaholic. This individual is not a myopic workhorse with blinders, keeping one-track focus on the fast lane, excluding family, friends, and even self in the race for early ulcers or a heart attack. We have found that there are specific traits and behaviors that separate these hyper-performers from the old concept of workaholics, or stressed-out people (SOPs).

In our work with individuals and corporations over the past 10 years we have noticed a distinct correlation between lack of control in the direction of one's life and an increased incidence of illness. We have noticed a number of traits that are characteristic of stressed-out people, though few have all of these traits. Such individuals:

1. Go through the motions
2. Manage time poorly
3. Are motivated externally, if at all
4. Seek safety and comfort rather than risks and challenges
5. Do things by the book instead of creatively
6. Often feel helpless or hopeless in the face of problems or difficulties
7. Are more likely to give up easily than persevere
8. Have low self-esteem and self-confidence, often blaming others

9. Have few, if any, distinct goals
10. Are generally pessimistic and guilty
11. Have many symptoms, and/or illness or diseases
12. Are past- or future-oriented
13. Are rigid and inflexible

Stressed-out people work long hours, seem to run madly from one place or task to another, yet never get everything done, and never seem on top of things. Eventually they run out of gas and may suffer job burnout. This is what was commonly thought to be a workaholic.

While SOPs may work extremely hard and long and may appear to be new workaholics, their work is a mask for one or more of these negative features. They may seek recognition and admiration for their long work hours and seeming dedication to their jobs, but the fact is that often they are inefficient and ineffective. They wear their work as a medal of sacrifice, their lack of a vacation as a symbol of dedication.

The true new workaholic would *rather* work than go on a trip to Mexico—or as the late Ansel Adams, a self-avowed workaholic, once said, "I like what I'm doing and this *is* my vacation."

Relaxation is essential. However, one misunderstood aspect of relaxation is equating it with leisure time or vacations. Relaxation for a new workaholic can be a business trip flying first class, or a business dinner in an elegant setting with excellent service.

William Theobald, a professor at Purdue University in Indiana, specializes in recreation studies. He was startled by the reaction of CEOs to the notion of leisure time. "The reaction from these CEOs, who usually work around 70 hours a week, [is] 'How could you possibly do that, let alone teach it?'"

Theobald has interviewed and socialized with some of this country's most successful high-level business executives. He found most to be happy, aware, and devoid of the unhealthy symptoms associated with stressed-out people. With his new-found perspective, Theobald initiated, through the university, a 10-year study of 60 CEOs identified as workaholics in 60 Fortune 500 companies. After the fourth year of the study Theobald had this to say: "So far I've found that most high-level executives prefer the boardroom to the Bahamas. They don't really enjoy leisure time; they feel their work is their leisure time."

Theobald's group enjoys the excitement and pace of work, and they possess a high level of energy. According to his findings, they sleep five to six hours per night and consider an early meeting to be 7 A.M., rather than 9 o'clock.

Theobald's findings cut across the grain of conventional thought regarding workaholics, who are usually referred to in negative terms. The term workaholic was first used by psychiatrists in the 1950s to describe the negative aspects of work-related stress and job burnout. The similarity of the term to alcoholic is not an accident. Individuals experiencing excessive work-related stress do have a high incidence of alcohol and drug abuse.

Robert, sales manager for a large domestic car dealership, works 10 hours a day and half a day on Saturdays. He earns about $40,000 a year and says he misses being on the "front line" selling cars. He is feared by most of the sales force for his tirades at sales meetings, and he blames his subordinates or his superiors when he fails to meet goals. Though he has told few people, Robert feels that he is not a very good manager.

Robert joins several of his colleagues for drinks practically every Friday evening, and returns home to his family late. He claims he has a good time on his evenings out, but he invariably regrets the hangover the morning after. He reluctantly admits he also stops for drinks several other nights each week after work.

Julie is the general manager for a radio station. She is an intense and demanding person, by her own description. She is respected by the station owner for her accomplishments and the profits she has brought in to the company; however, Julie has a difficult time maintaining relationships. She has been married twice, has one child and is presently a single mother. Julie is in therapy seeking to relate better to the men in her life and to stop her cocaine habit.

While Robert and Julie may seem to have some new-workaholic characteristics, in fact, they are people in crisis who have escaped into their work and into drug and alcohol abuse to avoid much of the unpleasantness in their lives. Though they work extremely long hours and occasionally produce valuable or even admirable results, they are really poor time managers and have low self-esteem. Their situations are examples of the SOP, not the new workaholic.

Both of these people are SOPs who have developed unhealthy and dangerous ways of coping with the negative aspects of their problems and with stress. It is unfortunate that the term workaholic has taken on such an unpleasant connotation. *Webster's New World Dictionary* treats the word more objectively. It defines a workaholic as a person possessing a compulsive need to work. We would amend that definition to "one who enjoys work with a passion, who truly equates work with pleasure, and is striving to please himself or herself rather than merely working for the money, promotion, or other outer directed motives."

Our work shows that new workaholics are not defined merely by the hours they work (though most do work more than the standard 40-hour week). They are defined by their attitude toward their work. Enjoyment and enthusiasm for their work are two traits that separate the new workaholic from the SOP. Yes, the money is nice, but that is not the prime motivator for new workaholics. In fact, quite often they do not measure their success in terms of money, but in terms of the successful accomplishment of some particular aspect of their work.

For a new-workaholic retail executive, today's success may be the successful negotiation of exclusive rights to a new product line. A new-workaholic actress would consider nomination by her peers for an Oscar as a measure of success. Certainly those successes may mean financial rewards as well, but it is not merely the money by which these individuals measure their achievements.

David Ben-Gurion, a former prime minister of Israel, has been quoted as saying, "I consider [work], as a human function, as a basis of human life, the most dignified thing in the life of a human being, and which ought to be free, creative, and I am proud of it."

Dr. Marilyn Machlowitz, who has written extensively about workaholics, comments, "There seems to be a very fine line between the highly motivated, energetic person and the workaholic."

It is the highly motivated, energetic, adaptable, inner directed people we call new workaholics. They are the hyper-performers, the high-level achievers who get things done. Have you ever heard the old saying, "If you want something done, give it to a busy person"? Not just any busy person; rather, we believe that bromide was referring to a new workaholic—a person who gets things done, right! We use the term hyper-performer and new workaholic interchangeably.

We have found 10 characteristics that are shared by new workaholics and optimal performers. Both groups are:

1. Passionate about their work
2. Adaptable
3. Centered in the present moment
4. Resourceful
5. Aware of their personal power
6. Persevering
7. Optimistic
8. Creative
9. Good at setting goals
10. Good at time management

This book and our workshops are specifically designed to develop and implement a program to enhance optimal performance and develop a winning pattern in your work life. Our plan is called the A.I.M. program and consists of *A*ctive relaxation as the foundation for managing excessive stress and preparing for effective *I*magery of the end result, and *M*ental rehearsal of the process of achieving the objective.

This book provides both the assessment device and an outline for developing customized organizational and individual A.I.M. programs. It is not enough to stay physically fit; to be successful and not suffer the ravages of stress, you must develop a regular program of Mental Fitness™.

Hyper-Performance Equals Success

Are you a hyper-performer? Do you work nine hours or more at least one day a week? Do you work one or more weekend days a month? Do you really like what you do, the joy of achieving and the thrill of accomplishment in your work? Those are characteristics of the movers and shakers of the world.

Some individuals who answer yes to these questions are Pope John Paul II, Margaret Thatcher, Bob Hope, Bill Marriott, David Rockefeller, Isaac Asimov, William Proxmire, and William McGowan, the founder of MCI, the long distance telephone company. Each one of these people is a self-proclaimed workaholic, or has been described as such by biographers.

The term workaholic is not a consistent, well defined term. The database of the National Library of Medicine does not list one clinical research study on workaholics. In our own work with corporate executives, professional athletes, and high-level performers we found three fundamental differences between these hyper-performers and SOPs: The new workaholics practiced stress management techniques; they had very little unexpressed anger; and they had control over their lives.

Where Are You on the Hyper-Performance Scale?

This book is more than an explanation of what we believe new workaholics are; it is a method by which readers may become hyper-performers, or sharpen those traits they already possess. To achieve any goal, you must first know where you currently are. As author Jim Cathcart says, "Prescription before diagnosis is malpractice." To develop your career and personal attributes, an assessment of your present status is essential.

It is valuable for executives to have methods to improve their own performance, but it is equally important for these executives to have more effective ways to evaluate and help subordinates become better performers and higher achievers, if those employees are motivated. This book provides both the method to evaluate present levels of performance and techniques to expand and enhance those levels.

In order to know what direction to take and what areas have the most room for enhancement, a point of reference is needed. We have developed and included several diagnostic tools that you can self-administer to give you a present reading. In a later chapter we provide the Personal Inventory Profile™ with which you can measure your present status in the 10 traits of a hyper-performer.

Are You a Hyper-Performer?

Here is a brief questionnaire to see if you are a hyper-performer.

Circle the most accurate answer:

YES/NO   1. I need less than eight hours sleep per night.

YES/NO   2. When I eat alone I read or work.

YES/NO   3. My work is the most fulfilling part of my life.

YES/NO   4. I am usually energetic.

YES/NO   5. I would work as much as I do now even if I were independently wealthy.

YES/NO   6. I can work any time.

YES/NO   7. I can work any place.

YES/NO   8. I consider my work to be my recreation.

YES/NO   9. I work more than 50 hours a week.

YES/NO   10. I have a daily "To Do" list.

YES/NO   11. I find retirement a dirty word.

YES/NO   12. It is not unusual for me to work on a weekend or holiday.

YES/NO   13. I am healthy.

YES/NO   14. I frequently cancel social appointments so I can get more work done.

YES/NO   15. I am basically happy.

YES/NO   16. I find distinctions between work and time off to be vague.

YES/NO   17. I prefer risk and challenge to smooth sailing.

YES/NO   18. I am in control of my life.

YES/NO   19. My work involvement causes problems for my family and friends.

YES/NO   20. I can easily go on to a new project before I complete the present one.

YES/NO   21. I am optimistic about life.

SCORING: 16 or more YES answers—You are a hyper-performer.

12–15—You are a borderline hyper-performer.

11 or less—You are presently not a hyper-performer.

To hyper-performers, job satisfaction—the feeling of accomplishment—is one avenue to happiness. As Theobald is finding in his study of the 60 CEOs, most are happy, alert, and without the symptoms and ill health that stress and overwork are supposed to cause.

For many nonworkaholics, work is perceived as injurious, and most certainly not healthy. That notion is incorrect. The Duke University Longitudinal Study of Aging found that job satisfaction and joy in one's work are the strongest predictors of longevity. A Georgetown University study found most top level executives do not keel over from overwork; in fact, they live longer than most people. What kills is not work. What does kill is not having control; when you are doing what you want to do you have control.

Control — A Crucial Element

Control over one's life direction or work life seems to be a critical factor that separates unhealthy, less effective people who suffer the damaging effects of excessive stress and overwork from new workaholics, who we have found are the high-level achievers, the hyper-performers. Control is essential for new workaholics to avoid illness.

The effects of loss of control over one's work life and environment are apparent in a client we counseled. Wayne had taken an action that snowballed. Soon he seemed to not only lose control, but he lost nearly everything that was meaningful to him. However, even in such extreme situations control can be regained and effectiveness reinstituted.

Wayne worked for a Department of Defense contractor. He was aware of gross negligence and deliberate misappropriation of materials by a senior supervisor. Wayne wrestled with his conscience and his obligations to his family. He finally decided he would report what he was aware of to the proper authorities even though he was quite certain doing so would jeopardize his career and could create havoc in his personal life.

All his darkest imaginings came true as the individual he reported viciously defended himself and vindictively attacked Wayne. Wayne was fired from his job, shunned by his friends, and in the course of the two years that the proceedings dragged on his wife divorced him. To say that he felt completely out of control is to only see the surface of his situation.

Wayne came to us for both medical help and psychological suturing.

It seemed to him that the entire government had turned its back on him, his company had swept him under the rug, and he was being abandoned by all the significant individuals in his life. He was taking antidepressant drugs; his thought patterns were so negatively channeled that only intensive medication prevented constant anticipatory anxiety attacks and very likely a complete nervous breakdown. He was a basket case.

The first intervention was to teach Wayne active relaxation. That became a difficult task. When not on his medication, he had very little ability to concentrate on anything other than his problems. We helped him with sessions designed to concentrate his attention on his breathing and on relaxing his body. After a few controlled sessions where we would take him through an active relaxation experience, he was able to gain enough control to lead himself into a relaxed state at home.

This provided Wayne with the first semblance of control he had experienced in over a year. This was an extreme case, but it points out the power of developing control in even one small area of one's life. From the point at which Wayne could relax himself, he was able to reduce and finally eliminate the antidepressant drugs. Again more control.

Then we worked on imagery of the end result desired. First Wayne had to get a grasp on what it was he wanted to happen in his life. He had to develop specific and realistic objectives. One of his first objectives was to pursue reinstatement in his job. Without being exonerated of the counter-charges levied by the person whose illegalities he had reported, he would forever live under the specter of his own undoing. Cleaning up his own mess became his major goal. His end-result imagery was of himself being congratulated for his courage in reporting the white collar crimes, and imagery of himself back at his old job and being respected for having persevered.

These were not easy images for Wayne to create and repeat as often as was prescribed. At first these images served to remind him of the ugly predicament he was in. Were it not for the active relaxation, he might well have slumped back into remorse, depression, and self-pity. But as the weeks passed he gained strength from his end-result imagery and began to consciously believe it could actually come about.

What the mind imagines, the body pursues. Wayne was able to mentally rehearse the steps he needed to take to have himself cleared of any wrongdoing. These included challenging the inaccurate and extremely negative evaluations given to him by the superior whom he had reported. Further, he rehearsed the presentation of his case before a board of inquiry. There were many other additional steps he needed to rehearse and then take.

It would be easy for people on the sidelines looking at Wayne's situation to simply say that he should have done this or that and maybe his situation wouldn't have ended up so rotten. True enough, he had made many tactical errors after he decided to blow the whistle, but the reactions he encountered, the procedures that were thrust upon him, and the cunning of the superior he reported were all extremely difficult to predict given the circumstances. As for his choice to blow the whistle in the first place, that was a moral decision that extracted more suffering than if he himself had chosen to steal from his company.

After many more months of gaining control over his personal life, and slowly taking the necessary administrative and legal steps, inch by inch Wayne nudged the truth from the rock it was hidden under. The supervisor was eventually fired and Wayne was exonerated and rehired. Some individuals still considered him persona non grata, and his wife was gone forever, but he changed his perception of those reactions as being indicative of weak relationships in the first place.

Today Wayne is in control of his life. He has received two promotions, and is clearly a stronger individual. As Wayne explains it, "The turnaround began with my being able to stop my negative thinking. I picked up momentum with each positive action I took to get my job back and get that stealing, lying s.o.b. out of there."

Setting goals, developing the personal power to achieve them, and having the perseverance to overcome the obstacles along the way are important traits of optimal performers.

It Is Not Work That Kills You

The results and conclusions of the Georgetown and Purdue University studies on work, stress, longevity, and health show that it is not work, even a lot of work, that has damaging effects. Satisfaction and joy with one's accomplishments and success actually increase life expectancy and seem to promote health. This is a conclusion we have come to also, and it leads to the next point, that stress and hyper-performance are not synonymous.

executives are also prone to heart attacks and other illnesses. In our rapidly changing society and fast-paced life, with changes in family structure, sexual roles, economic situations, and social scenes, our bodies/minds/spirits are bombarded by demands to adjust and respond.

Selye described our body's efforts to accommodate distress as the general adaptation syndrome. This syndrome has three stages: the alarm reaction, the resistance stage, and the exhaustion stage. The alarm reaction is what has been called the "fight or flight" response. It is usually a brief period of reaction to a specific situation. When our prehistoric ancestors encountered some dangerous or exhilarating event, fear of a sabre-toothed tiger or delight at a tasty-looking herd of some savory roast, the rush of adrenaline provided the needed burst of energy to flee or pursue dinner. But this biochemical response seldom lasted long.

Modern society has little use for the alarm reaction, but when emotional, psychological, or physical stressors tax our minds and bodies for long periods, the internal alarm continues and creates the need for resistance to the effects of the alarm reaction. What does the alarm reaction do to the body? In response to a "fight or flight" situation the body undergoes physical changes. The pupils dilate, blood vessels constrict flow to nonvital organs, sweat is produced, the liver releases glucose, the heart beats faster, and many other changes occur. These are survival reactions that are essential for emergencies, but when these changes persist the body must resist the adverse effects. This is the resistance stage.

Being remarkably resilient creatures, we can recover from the resistance stage once the stressing agents and the alarm reactions are removed. However, when the stress continues beyond a point, exhaustion sets in and that is when the body's immune system begins to deteriorate. With the immune system weakening, the body becomes a progressively easier target for viruses and bacteria.

When the exhaustion stage has been reached, the body can no longer spring back like a sapling. Instead the body, like an old tree that has spent years in the path of a howling wind, becomes bent, worn, and may die an early death. Melodramatic, you may say, but the truth is that with each passing year increasing research shows that stress plays an important role in such diverse disease and chronic conditions as cancer, heart disease, arthritis, psoriasis, back pain, headaches, and colitis.

It is important to recognize that people who are happy, working long and hard, and who enjoy their work intensity are not necessarily suffering from the adverse effects of stress. Hyper-performance is not synonymous with being overstressed. We must not equate overworked and overstressed people with new workaholics.

Stress develops from all areas of our lives. Even new workaholics are not spared the possibility of stress from family relationships, financial catastrophes, physical injuries, traffic jams, screwy flight schedules, bad food, and a long list of aggravations. In fact, even joyous events cause stress: purchase of a new home, vacations, Christmas, marriage, and pregnancy.

The Importance of Stress Management

Increasingly, people suffer from diseases of adaptation, such as peptic ulcers, heart disease, anxiety, and high blood pressure. Loneliness and isolation for some people bring about a loss of meaning and personal worth. The resulting lack of stimulation causes diseases of stagnation, such as depression and digestive disturbances.

If an individual does not have effective coping devices for the stresses of contemporary life, these demands and stresses can lead to physical, emotional, and behavioral symptoms. And, of course, if allowed to continue, those symptoms will affect one's work performance, relationships, and physical well being. The cycle will continue because those burdens will add even more stresses of their own; the cycle goes around and around with increasing velocity until the individual breaks down physically, psychologically, or both.

We have found the most effective coping mechanism for life's stresses is active relaxation practiced on a regular, frequent basis.

As we have said, stress builds up to a point where performance begins to decrease. The first sign of this is usually self-observed. You notice that you are not able to do what you'd like to do the way you'd like to do it. Then, the stress begins to show up in emotional and physical symptoms. It is becoming more and more difficult to separate the psychological and physical symptoms because they are interrelated. For example, migraine headaches are certainly physical; heat-sensitive instruments able to detect painful areas of the body

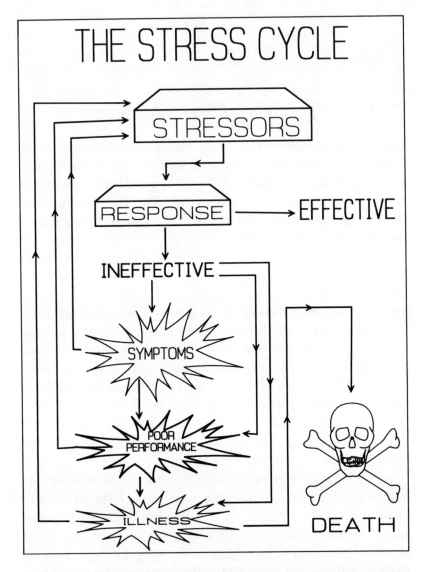

FIGURE 1. Stressors require the individual to elicit a response. If the response is effective, the stress cycle is broken before it gets a chance to start. If it is ineffective, however, symptoms, impairment of performance, and illness can develop. Persistence in this cycle can lead to death.

have graphically shown the presence of migraines. Yet a migraine can be caused by emotional factors, which in turn can lead to psychological reactions such as depression, and behavioral changes such as short-temper, drug abuse, and absenteeism.

One strength of high-level achievers and highly successful new workaholics is their ability to manage and control stress. Whether the stress originates at home, in personal relationships, or anyplace else, optimal performers are able to vent stress in healthy, effective ways.

Philip is an example. He owns a highly productive, successful advertising agency employing 15 people and generating $25 million in sales a year. Philip is well liked by his employees, who are motivated by his personal spirit and drive. His colleagues respect Philip for his professional accomplishments, for which he has won three national awards from his industry's trade association.

On weekends, Philip plays jazz clarinet with a group of amateur musicians. He also attends his daughter's softball games and plays poker twice a month. Philip works about 50 hours a week, not extremely long hours, plus an occasional one- or two-day business trip. In many regards Philip appears to have an ideal life. He is currently divorced and has two sons, 19 and 21, and he shares custody with his ex-wife of their 13-year-old daughter.

He is one of the most creative, productive, and well rounded people his friends know. But one of his sons is a heroin addict and a convicted felon. Philip was devastated when his son was arrested for attempted murder, and in the weeks that followed he was shocked and then numbed as the details of his son's recent life were revealed.

The ordeal for Philip and his son is not over. He is devoting innumerable hours and resources to helping his son overcome one of the most addictive substances imaginable. Yet, through all of his personal trauma and pain, he retains his creativity and personal levels of excellence.

When asked, Philip will quickly credit optimism and stress management in his life, his workouts with the punching bag, and his quiet moments of imagery alone each and every day with preserving his sanity and his physical health.

"If it weren't for the [canvas punching bag] and my 15 or 20 minutes of deep relaxation each day, I'd be a wreck," he says. "I've been working out with the bag since college and I started the relaxation when I brought in a stress consultant for my entire staff a few years ago. The day that I learned Tim was an addict I must have done over an hour on the bag till my knuckles were bleeding into the gloves and I fell like a sack of laundry to the floor. I was a mess for two, maybe three weeks till I realized I wasn't to blame and I still had my own life to keep moving forward if I was going to help Tim."

The A.I.M. Strategy for Mental Fitness™

In our work with new workaholics and, conversely, with SOPs, we have discovered specific techniques that will lead individuals out of the quagmire of overstress and SOP characteristics and toward the achievement of excellence. We have studied the features of optimal performers and high achievers. There are common skills and methods they use in their everyday lives to enhance or maintain their winning styles.

These skills can be learned by anyone willing to put in the effort. They can be started immediately and their effects are cumulative. The A.I.M. program begins with *Active relaxation*. Through active relaxation you are able to avoid the harmful, illness-causing effects of excessive stress. Active relaxation is essential to managing stress, to keeping a clear mind and preparing yourself for imagery and mental rehearsal.

*I*magery of your goals and objectives is the second strategy in the program. It is composed of imagery of the end result and rehearsal imagery of the goal-achievement process. Imagery of the end result of your goals puts your unconscious mind to work toward your goals.

*M*ental rehearsal of the process of achieving your goals is real practice of professional and mental skills. All of these together form a tremendous momentum of conscious and unconscious personal force.

This program is designed to produce immediate results as well as long-term benefits. World-class athletes, corporate

executives, entrepreneurs, artists, musicians, and professionals in any field can and have used the A.I.M. program to
achieve or enhance their personal and professional success.
These skills generate a tremendous momentum of conscious
and unconscious personal force that will propel you toward
success.

2

The 10 Traits of Optimal Performers

*E*arlier, we identified 10 characteristics of hyper-performers. We observed that as these traits develop, performance and achievement increase.

The 10 traits are:

1. Passion and enthusiasm
2. Adaptability
3. Being centered in the present moment
4. Resourcefulness
5. Personal power
6. Perseverance
7. Optimism
8. Creativity
9. Goal setting
10. Time efficiency

Now let us describe what each of these means and how each fits into the new workaholic's life.

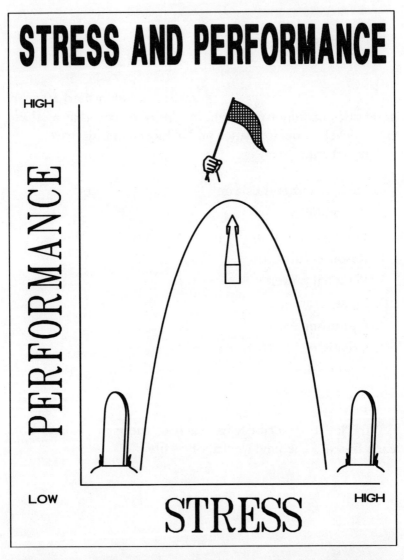

FIGURE 2. An optimal level of stress produces high-level performance. At higher and lower stress levels performance decreases. As suggested by the tombstones at each end of the stress-performance curve, too much or too little stress can kill the individual.

Passion

The first trait is passion. There are several synonyms for passion: commitment, energy, and enthusiasm. Ralph Waldo Emerson once said, "Nothing great was ever achieved without enthusiasm," and the philosopher Hegel commented, "Nothing great in the world was accomplished without passion." We believe that passion is the cornerstone to becoming a hyper-performer.

How can you infuse passion into your work? If you lack enthusiasm, it may be developed by changing your perspective on work using the imagery we will explain later, such as re-evaluations of your present career and a mental change in your attitude toward it, or by finding what work you can become passionate about, and then changing your career.

Bill had been a contractor for over 12 years, and though he worked hard, had done well, and had earned an adequate living for himself and his family, he increasingly felt his work was a grind. He knew that one of the reasons his business was not doing as well as he'd wished was because he was not very enthused. His lack of enthusiasm was felt by his employees, who in turn displayed an equal lack of energy. Morale was at an all-time low and Bill wanted out.

He discussed his feelings with his wife. She knew that he really wanted to open a restaurant. A fool's choice of business is what most of Bill's friends thought of the idea. Better to stay with what you know, in construction, they advised, than venture into the restaurant arena. Still, with his wife's encouragement and help he found a nostalgic location in a dilapidated bar on Broadway in the downtown section of his town, and after comparing it with 50 other sites he settled on it in spite of the major renovation it would require.

Bill envisioned it to be a businessmen's bar and restaurant that would cater to political, business, and theater trade for both lunches and dinner. He used his construction loan contacts for financing and his own building know-how for renovation. Bill and his crew changed the dark blue interior into a rich oak paneling and stained-glass motif. He brought a chef from France to manage the restaurant's food preparation and was delighted to find the business successful within a year.

To what does he credit his success in a business that is usually fraught with failure? "First, location. Second, the food has to be great and the service flawless. But for long-term success, either myself or somebody in my family who works as hard as I do has to be here all the time," Bill says. His wife works by his side in the restaurant. "Otherwise, I'd probably never get to spend time with her," he adds.

However, when he speaks of his new business his eyes flash with excitement and enthusiasm. The long hours, 10 A.M. to 1 A.M. the following day, are no problem for him or his wife. They love their work and, now in their third year, they are ringing up substantial financial rewards as well as emotional ones. Was it a risk? Could they have failed? Did the career change breathe new life into him and his wife? The answer is yes to all those questions. Would such a dramatic change be right for you or another person? Certainly it is one option among many.

Management World magazine published a study for which they interviewed two groups of people. The first group were high-level personnel executives and high-level managers. The second were graduates of business schools. The researchers asked these two groups what traits they thought would most help an individual get a good job; there was one characteristic both the managers and the graduates agreed on: enthusiasm.

The salesperson who has limited professional skills and little technical product knowledge, but who has obvious and contagious enthusiasm, will sell more than one who has the former skills but lacks enthusiasm. Think for a moment about your own present situation. Are you enthusiastic, passionate, excited about your work?

Adaptability

The second trait is adaptability. Being adaptable is related to your ability to handle stress, because a major stressful time occurs when we are called upon to change. New workaholics not only have the capacity to adjust to change but to actually thrive on it. Inherent in this trait is the ability to take risks and to step out of that invisible shell we have around us that is our comfort zone. These comfort zones are powerful inhibitors to adaptation and change. You may not even realize how much your behavior is influenced by them.

Take a moment to try two small experiments. First, fold your hands in the natural way you would if you were sitting at a desk. Look at your hands and notice which thumb is on top. Now refold your hands so that the other thumb is on top and change the other fingers to correspond. Does the reversed position feel strange to you?

Now fold your arms just as you might while standing waiting in line. Notice how your arms are folded, left over right or right over left. Consciously reverse your arms so that the opposite arm is on top. You may even find this a bit awkward to accomplish the first time. Though these are not very risky treks outside of your comfort zone, for most people it feels a bit odd to step out just this little bit. You can imagine how difficult it can be for some people to make a career step out of what they feel comfortable with, or to make a decision that departs significantly from secure ground.

We become so involved in our comfort zones that we don't want to leave them. For example, do you eat the same foods for lunch or go to the same restaurants often? And can you identify the comfort zones in your decision-making process? The tendency to stay within routines, and patterns of behavior and thinking in which we are comfortable can be very limiting. Additionally, such rigidity can produce its own stress as problems and situations occur for which change and adaptability must be part of the solution. Often the more we resist change, the more we increase our stress levels.

High-level achievers know that change and the risks that may accompany change are not only necessary but vital to success and accomplishment. Letting go of the fear of failure and being open to risk will allow you to become more adaptable. Change is an inevitable part of life and resisting it can be unhealthy to both corporate and corporeal bodies. As Richard Bach points out in *Illusions,* "What the caterpillar calls the end of the world, the Master calls a butterfly."

How do you view change in your life? Do you feel uncomfortable with calculated risks that have some possibility of failure? There is no risk if the change is so safe that failure is not possible or is extremely remote. Are you afraid to take a chance and try something that is unproven? Fear is the major inhibitor to change and yet we are born with only two fears: the fear of falling and the fear of loud noises. All other fears are developed after birth.

As Denis Waitley in *Seeds of Greatness,* suggests, the word *fear* can be thought of as an acronym for False Evidence Appearing Real. Several studies show that the single most common fear affecting people in the United States is the fear of public speaking. And what is the great danger in giving a public speech or presentation to a group? What is the great risk, the great consequence in speaking publicly? Well, it certainly is not among the major causes of death or injury.

If the underlying fear in public speaking is fear of embarrassment, failure, or ridicule, these are not catastrophic or deadly. Yet we suspect that fear of being thought a failure, stupid, clumsy, or other embarrassments is at the root of many individuals' resistance to change. And if you think about why you are afraid, you may realize that what you are afraid of might not happen at all. Simplistic as it may sound, most terrible things you might envision as a result of a proposed change never happen. Are you resisting change because of false evidence that *appears* real?

Change may take the form of a new career, as Bill chose. Or, it may mean more frequent but less dramatic changes, such as a new diagnostic procedure, a new product or service, spending more money than last year on marketing or advertising, taking a new position regarding a labor dispute, putting a new but promising person in a role of added responsibility instead of keeping the status quo; in short, taking any action that leads you out of your comfort zone. Become more aware of your mental and physical comfort zones by writing them down as you notice them. Only then can you work on dissolving them if you choose.

Present-Centered

The next characteristic is being centered in the present moment. The opposite of this is living in the past or the future. Living in the moment is a buzzword, a concept that gained attention in the 1970s in the form of "live for now, the bomb may drop tomorrow." Being present-centered mentally is valuable and important. Often people become present-centered at important or crucial times. We usually learn through trial and error that if we don't pay attention we may miss something essential in a meeting, in negotiations, or even in our reading. You may remember yourself in grade school being called on by the teacher to answer a question after having been distracted. It is an embarrassing situation that does not promote successful outcomes.

Do you recall in the 1984 Summer Olympics, when Mary Lou Retton needed a 9.9 in the vault to win the gold medal and she made a 10.0? Do you think she was in the present moment when she was executing that vault? You can be certain she was not wondering what she was going to have for dinner that night, nor about a movie she might have seen a month before. She was 100 percent in that moment of competition.

Being present-centered means your dominant thoughts are about what is going on right now rather than dwelling on past successes or failures or future worries and possibilities. This is not to say that you might not look to the past for insight or learning. But living in the past lacks something. As the last elephant in the parade knows, hindsight may show you the way to go, but it is rarely inspiring.

Likewise, living for the future or constantly wishing for things to change gets you nowhere. Live your life creating change in the direction in which you wish to arrive.

New workaholics deal with problems that are now, situations and conditions that exist presently. For example, if you are in a meeting with a colleague or associate, you will be more effective, productive, and creative if your thoughts are solely concerned with the conversation and issues of that moment. Thinking about something that person did or said a month ago that upset you, or thinking about what might happen next week, is not going to help you deal with the present.

We're reminded of the amusing story of the elderly couple who went to a therapist for marital counseling. When asked how long they had been married they responded, "For 54 years." And when asked how long they had been having problems they said, "For 52 years." "Why in heaven's sake did you wait so long?" the therapist asked. "We wanted to wait till the children died," they said. Now, that's living too much for the future.

Being centered in the present moment is something you need to check yourself for frequently. In the greatest measure, hyper-performers in all endeavors keep their dominant thoughts and attention in the present moment.

The focus and intensity generated by being in the moment as completely as possible is a benefit with practical application. An example of how present-centering created a positive result concerns a colleague of ours, David, who many years ago was asked to testify as an expert witness at a murder trial.

The attorney who hired David had heard him speak once at a luncheon, but didn't know that he had never been before a jury as a witness. David recognized his lack of experience in testifying and in answering questions a prosecuting attorney might ask. He practiced 15 minutes of relaxation and imagery each day and imagined himself calm on the witness stand, totally in the moment of the courtroom, relaxed in answering questions, and confident in his professional experience.

David's stint as an expert witness went smoothly and he handled himself well even under some challenging questions. After that one court appearance David's reputation as an expert witness developed and a significant increase in his professional stature and income resulted. In fact, the prosecuting attorney in the case later asked David how many years he had been an expert witness and couldn't believe it was his first time.

Keeping your awareness and focus in the present is a powerful enhancement in itself. Much as laser light is powerful because it is focused, you become more effective as you become more focused on the present events and actions that you are involved in.

Resourcefulness

The fourth characteristic is resourcefulness. This is a positive resourcefulness, constructive and imaginative, the ability to gather resources to accomplish goals and create solutions. This trait in new workaholics allows them to bring together people, relationships, financial capital, organizational skills, material, ideas, and much more to assist in getting the job done. Hyper-performers are able to listen to helpful information and consider for use what others might overlook or disregard. By being aware and open to new possibilities you aid in your own resourcefulness.

A recent television series, *MacGyver,* is about a special agent hired to do impossible missions for the government. MacGyver survives each episode because he uses simple, common items found wherever he might be to save his life and escape or capture the bad guys. His resourcefulness alone is his success; he carries no gun and uses no sophisticated technology, only himself and his mind. High-level achievers are not held back by an empty cupboard or lack of capital. They find what they need and create their own opportunities.

Personal Power

Realization of one's personal power is the next trait. Personal power refers to the ability to influence the environment and conditions around us. We all have personal power, whether we choose to exercise it or not. Personal power is different from people who have power. We assume that individuals have political, financial, or social power by virtue of elected office, financial resources, or celebrity. That is not always the case, nor do those apparent power bases always yield personal power.

Personal power is connected to those attributes that are distinctly your own. Your personality, the alliances you have, or the information you control make up the foundations of personal power. These elements allow you to influence outcomes and create new choices.

In his book, *You Can Negotiate Anything*, Herbert Cohen describes a person who is seemingly without any personal power. He shows how even a prisoner in a high security prison may be able to develop some personal power to negotiate for a cigarette. The guard is smoking a cigarette in the hall outside the prisoner's cell. The prisoner calls the guard over and asks for a cigarette. The guard says, "Why should I give you a cigarette? You have no money, nothing to trade for it."

The prisoner looks the guard directly in the eyes and says, "If you don't give me a cigarette I'll smash my head against the walls and scream that you beat me. They may not believe me, but you'll have a lot of paperwork to fill out, anyway, just for one lousy cigarette." The guard gives him a smoke.

Despite the hyperbole of the situation the story points out a truism of personal power: If you don't use it, you lose it. The prisoner's power hinged upon the degree of certainty he instilled in the guard that he would carry out his threat to bloody his head and scream.

Personal power in sales is extremely valuable. Some salespeople believe they have little personal power, that they must succeed because of the benevolence of buyers. However, that is not true of Frank, a jewelry salesman in New York. He calls on retail jewelry stores as a representative for an expensive line of rings, watches, and pendants. Most salespeople come in and open up a vast array of products, from which the buyer selects what he or she believes will sell well.

Frank has a different style. He arrives very nattily dressed with a flat, handsome, black leather jewelry case held on fingertips chest high, as a waiter might carry a small tray of appetizers. After exchanging greetings, Frank mentions that he has some special selections to show the buyer. He explains to the buyer that what he has in his case are rare finds, unusual designs, selected specifically for that store and its clientele.

Frank may even open the case just a crack and nearly peek in as he describes some wonderful diamond ring or gold pendant. Before too many minutes pass, the customer is curious to see what is in the case. At about that point Frank begins talking about something else. Even though he has repeated this sales pattern for many years with the same customers they still become curious to see what's in the case. When the customer's curiosity is fully piqued, Frank is in control because he has created a desire in the customer to see the merchandise, and he has used his ability to control the viewing of that merchandise as part of his personal power.

Sometimes it is not the strength of your personality that creates personal power but your knowledge. Perhaps you have cultivated a breadth of knowledge about your industry that few people have. You may have specific technical knowledge that you have developed from your own research. Maybe you know who the important players are in a developing merger or land development. That knowledge can be a source of personal power. However, it is only power when you exercise it.

Richard Bach realized the importance of testing and stretching your personal power when he said, "Argue for your limitations and they're yours." When we present limitations as arguments for not exercising our power to get things done, we do indeed own those limitations.

An effective way to increase your personal power is to take an inventory of the areas of knowledge, professional and personal experience, contacts, and strengths within your personality and lifestyle. From this inventory you can imagine the various possibilities that exist for developing your personal power.

Another aspect of your personal power is the effect you have on others. Are people happy or comfortable when they are around you? A compliment from you to an associate or subordinate can have a powerful effect that can elicit a positive response. In *The One Minute Manager,* the authors say personal power is not really flexing power. Power comes, they say, in catching people doing something right and then affirming their actions or ideas.

The characteristics of inner direction and self-esteem are inherent components of personal power. Self-esteem and good feelings about yourself usually create inner direction. When you feel you are a valuable person you are less motivated by the opinions and expectations of others and you are more comfortable with your own choices. New workaholics derive their motivation from within. External motivation can be strong, but it doesn't have any staying power.

The short-lived power of external motivation is humorously illustrated by the old story of the wealthy, aging Texas oilman who invites his most promising executives to his mansion. Leading them to his massive swimming pool he challenges them. "I have filled this pool with hungry piranha, crocodiles, sharks, and poisonous fish of all sorts. Whichever one of you swims across the pool and survives has your choice of 10 square miles of my best cattle-grazing land and the oil field beneath, 10 million dollars in cash, or the hand of my beautiful daughter who is heir to my fortunes."

Just as he finishes that speech, there is a splash in the pool, a flutter of activity, and a blur of speed as one of the young men jackknifes out of the other end of the pool, his suit slightly ripped but without a drop of blood. The old gentleman congratulates him and asks if he wants the 10 acres of land. The young man breathes deeply and shakes his head "no." "Do you want the 10 million?" the older man asks. Again a shake of the head. "Then you must want to marry my daughter," the old man says. A third shake of the head. "What then do you want?" he asks. The young man replies, "I just want to know who pushed me in the pool."

That is an example of external motivation. It will get you through a crisis, but it will not get you successfully through life. The joy of achievement, the inner gratification of a job well done, the personal satisfaction of having been your own motivator spins the gyroscope of inner direction for new workaholics. Nonworkaholics work hard for praise from their boss, to earn more money, or to meet a deadline, while new workaholics work because they enjoy the satisfaction of doing the job well. "The deepest principle in human nature is the craving to be appreciated," said philosopher William James. When you appreciate yourself you will never run out of motivation.

Expect powerful actions from yourself. Expectation leads to action. Robert Rosenthal conducted a study with a group of teachers who were told that a group of students were given a battery of tests to determine their IQs. Then certain students were identified, to the teachers only, as "bloomers" with the highest IQs. The teachers were told that these particular students tested highest and were expected to learn very well. In fact, the students identified to the teachers as "bloomers" were a mixture of average and higher IQs.

When the students finished the course, written reports were received from the teachers in addition to the grades and the following was found:

1. The students designated as bloomers uniformly received higher grades than the others.

2. This same group of students received the best personality ratings.

3. The worst personality ratings went to the students who were misclassified—those who had high IQs and learned a lot, but who weren't supposed to. (This may have a great bearing in organizations where individuals may be called hostile, aggressive, or not good team players.)

4. Those students who were classified as bloomers had an average increase of 6 points in their IQ when they were retested. They were apparently influenced by the conviction and expectation of their teachers.

A similar study was conducted with factory workers. Some with poor work histories were identified to supervisors as good employees expected to learn quickly and do well. Again, as with the students and teachers, only the supervisors were informed of the designations. And as with the students, those expected to do well, did extremely well. The implications of this expectancy factor is valuable both at the management level and at the personal growth level. If you expect powerful actions from yourself, you are more likely to live up to that expectation.

Perseverance

Perseverance is the sixth trait. A story is told about Beethoven, who was playing the piano for a small group of people. After he played, a woman said to him, "I just wish I could play that beautifully, I just wish I had been born with the gift of genius you have to play piano." To this, Beethoven replied, "If you had spent 40 years playing piano eight hours a day, as I have, then you, too, would have been born with this gift of genius."

Most winners win because they persevere in doing what losers would not even begin doing in the first place. Peter Drucker observes that all successful entrepreneurs he has met have in common a commitment to the systematic practice of innovation, rather than a certain type of personality. Practice, repeated effort even in the face of little or no observable progress, is what makes instant success. Goethe wrote, "The most important thing in life is to have great aim and to possess the aptitude and the perseverance to attain your objective."

Success comes from a persistent search for the right formula, the best combinations, the right product, the right market. Success is a game of inches. Like the Chinese proverb that a journey of a thousand miles begins with one step, no one single action is clinching. Hundreds of actions piled upon one another are what move you toward your objectives. And as Og Mandino suggests, with all the bends and twists in the road, we must persist because around the next bend, the next turn in our journey, may be the goal we seek.

Optimism

Optimism is the seventh characteristic winners possess. Harvey Firestone, the tire magnate, once commented that optimism and enthusiasm for an organization are like lubricants that help overcome friction. Allan Cox, in his book *The Making of the Achiever,* said that "Thinking positively is not a legislated experience, that is, you can't practice it merely because someone tells you to. You can't have it in one part of your life, for example, in your social life, but exclude it from work. Rather, optimism is the lifestyle-wide mental capacity to seek and find workable, beneficial options."

Optimism keeps you open to new options even when the tide is running against you. This is not to say that you must be optimistic all the time, or that you won't have a down day once in a while. The key is to have an overall optimism toward life. We've all heard about the difference in perspectives evidenced by viewing a glass as either half full or half empty, or by seeing the weather as partly cloudy or partly sunny. You can immediately begin adding optimism in your life through the language you use.

The self-fulfilling prophecy is never more applicable than when it comes to determining how you feel. Have a generally optimistic attitude and you will attract positive events and actions. Also, optimism leads to health, while pessimism leads to disease.

If you were discussing the current status of a project you are working on you might describe the situation as "I've run into a roadblock." A more optimistic approach might be, "I uncovered an interesting hurdle." It is very natural for someone to believe that this is merely a matter of semantics or word games, but the effects are not superficial. Your positive, optimistic language sets up unconscious objectives that are as powerful as your conscious ones. With practice you will be able to use your language to develop action plans for your goals.

Another effective way to create and maintain optimism is by smiling. The next time you feel a bit low decide that you will meet everyone that day with a smile regardless of the circumstances. Then notice closely how you are greeted and treated in return. Also, take note of how you feel when the day is over. Most likely you will notice a positive difference.

Creativity

The eighth characteristic of the new workaholic is the expression of creativity. Everyone is creative to some extent. Some choose not to express their creativity, however. There is a common misconception that creativity is the realm of artists: musicians, painters, writers, and photographers. However, every profession and endeavor not only has the capacity for, but requires, creativity. The executive responsible for finance, the manager responsible for productivity, the secretary responsible for file retrieval all have creative potential. When we lack the awareness of the need to be creative in our work, we also ignore the development of our creativity.

The first stage in being creative is being open to as much information and as many options as possible. A good definition of creativity is the joining of two or more ideas, actions, or possibilities to form a new outcome. While the notion that there is nothing new under the sun may be true, there are an infinite number of ways in which what already exists can be recombined.

The second stage of creativity is called incubation. After the work is finished let it percolate in your unconscious mind. During this stage creative people must allow themselves time for ambiguity, the situation in which not everything has to be clear and complete. Charles Garfield, in his book on peak performance, explains that optimal performers have an ability to tolerate ambiguity. That relates well to creativity. We see that new workaholics must be able to allow a project or idea to rest unresolved, ambiguous for a time until a creative solution develops.

After you have done all the spade work, the probing and gathering of information, you must allow time for fermentation. People who know a lot about a lot of things are often the most likely to put two widely different ideas together for a creative solution. More information is often the key to solving a problem. However, real creativity is often manifested by dropping the topic, clearing your mind, and waiting for the bulb to light up. This development is often done in the unconscious.

As we have said, creativity is not the dominion only of the arts. Salespeople, financiers, farmers, scientists, attorneys, marketers, and individuals in virtually any profession or avocation can employ creativity. For example, the president of a small environmental cleanup firm created an innovative promotional program.

He sent the CEOs of 70 of the nation's largest chemical firms a glossy photograph of a man in a white protective hooded suit used by toxic waste cleanup technicians. With long pincerlike tongs the eerie-looking fellow was pulling something out of a large pond of bubbling, steamy muck. On closer examination it was clear that what he was extracting from the goo was the most recent issue of that CEO's annual report to the stockholders. A short note suggested that what was represented in the photograph could be avoided by calling the telephone number provided. Results: Forty-two of the 70 CEOs called within two days of receipt. That's creative and effective.

Goal Setting

Goal setting is the ninth trait. Do you know why most people don't reach their goals? They don't reach them because they don't set any, at least not effective ones. Effective goals are specific, ideas of success, not general ones like a promotion sometime in the future, or to be happy, rich, or famous. What do those mean? They are too vague.

New workaholics have very specific goals and specific time periods for each of them. What we mean by specific periods is a goal such as Lee Iacocca had: to be vice president of Ford Motor Company by the age of 35. He made that his goal fully a dozen years before he actually achieved it, a few months late, at age 36.

Setting effective goals and objectives are the fodder for imagery to feed upon. The operative word in the last sentence is effective. We estimate that 9 of 10 individuals you ask will tell you that, indeed, they have set goals for themselves. But when the truth is examined, we would see that most goals people set are ineffective.

Setting the most effective goals possible is the kingpin to making the A.I.M. plan successful for you.

End-result imagery's success is enhanced or impeded by how specific the goal is. An example of fuzzy goals in a business environment is Bill, whose goal it is to be in management someday. With that as an objective, even using imagery and active relaxation, there is too little meat to make a sandwich. We would see a specific objective for Bill as having 40 people report to him as production manager of two plants with a salary of $55,000 within five years.

That would give Bill something he can really develop in his imagery. He can see himself behind the production manager's desk; walking through the plant with his assistant just as the production manager now does; and receiving his paycheck for $4500 each month. Those are the types of end-result imagery that have specific definition and riflelike accuracy.

Goals are the end result you're trying to achieve and end-result imagery is imagining with all your senses that the result has already been achieved. Suppose for a moment that your goal is to assist others in benefiting from this book. If you are a CEO and have 15 managers, you might imagine a meeting of those managers discussing the merits of this book, how much more effective the managers are, and how much better they understand themselves and each other in the context of their business and personal relationships. Imagine the sounds of the room, the voices; imagine the feel of the desk, the feeling you have about the individuals present.

Or, let's suppose that you are an entrepreneur and owner of a mail-order business with 10 employees. Your objective is to increase sales in the next quarter by $145,000 over last year's sales. You might imagine your accountant handing you the quarterly profit and loss statements and seeing the exact figures that would be $145,000 over last year's sales.

Further, you might imagine that you are enjoying sailing on the lake in your new boat you have bought with some of the additional money you have earned, or a new car, new clothes, whatever would be most pleasing to you. Spend a few sessions imagining yourself being interviewed by a trade journal about your resounding sales gains for your targeted

Characteristics of the
HYPER-PERFORMER

1. PASSION
2. PRESENT
3. POWER
4. PERSEVERE
5. CREATIVE
6. ADAPTABLE
7. RESOURCEFUL
8. OPTIMISTIC
9. GOALS
10. TIME

FIGURE 3.

quarter. Other images could be of writing out bonus checks or raises for those employees who were most involved in increasing sales.

If you are an account executive or sales manager you might effectively create a dollar amount goal and express that dollar objective in terms of units sold, additional units over the previous calendar period, a specific contract award, or any aspect that will reflect the dollar objective. You might imagine yourself obtaining a client's signature on a substantial contract, or imagine a victory celebration with your friends for achieving your sales goal. The more images you can devise the more you will enlist your unconscious in working toward achieving the end result.

The powerful quality of imagery of effective goals is that it utilizes the unconscious to select from the many options available day-to-day, those physical, emotional, environmental, and intellectual actions that lead most directly toward those mentally pictured goals. It is the cumulation of those small daily choices we make that result in achieving our objectives or not.

The Hidden Agenda

There can be a difference between our rhetorical goals and our true goals. Often executives become focused on the form or rhetoric of goals rather than the content or function. For example, in *Making of the Achiever* Allan Cox believes that corporations have values and wisdom of their own. While a manager may have a specific goal, say improving plant efficiency while cutting costs by specific measures, the deeper unconscious goal of that individual may be to establish his or her authority while appearing to be a person of action. Such goals may run counter to corporate objectives and constitute what can be called a hidden agenda.

Goals and Purpose Equal Health and Survival

Viktor Frankl, a noted Viennese psychiatrist and author of *Man's Search for Meaning,* found while a prisoner in a Nazi concentration camp that the survivors in his camp were those who had some overriding sense of purpose or goal in their lives. Even those men whose goals were revenge against the guards who had mistreated them had a better mental outlook and a higher rate of survival than captives who had no goals whatsoever.

An old seaman's adage says that a ship without a destination has no favorable wind. If your goals—your destinations—are not clear, you will be wasting time sailing to needless ports that collectively lead you nowhere. If your destination is well defined, then even efforts that do not reach the mark are more likely to yield some benefit toward reaching your goal.

In setting your goals do not hesitate to set them high; however, they should be attainable. If you are a middle manager working for Hewlett-Packard, a goal of being a vice president in the corporation may be lofty but in line with your career. On the other hand, if you are a general sales manager desiring to be a computer systems engineer, then perhaps you should consider the major shift in your career closely. What education and career path will get you there? If working with computers is your objective, then perhaps you would do better to play from your strengths and adjust your goal. You might set your sights on being a vice president of marketing in a major computer company, for example.

You would do well, however, to also set intermediate goals. For example, Gloria's goal is to become a state Supreme Court judge by age 40. This was her goal before she finished law school. If that were her only goal it is possible that she would become frustrated and perhaps even lose track of her ultimate destination in a few years.

However, Gloria had several intermediate goals. She planned to be working for an established law firm within a year after passing her bar exam. She actually achieved this even before she had the results of her second attempt at passing the exam (which she did pass). Her next goal is to become a partner in the firm and then run for a local judge's seat by the time she is 34. Each of her intermediate goals led her in the direction of her ultimate destination.

The value of such intermediate goals is the satisfaction gained from achieving them. Achieving intermediate goals creates a positive success habit and sets your unconscious mind to work toward solving problems and creating actions that take you closer to your larger objective.

Your goal-setting is most effective if you write your desires in clear, detailed fashion. This is true of both ultimate and intermediate goals. The written goal plan and action plan for reaching your objectives form a personal contract.

Time Management

The tenth characteristic of high-level achievers is that of time management. Have you ever wanted to save time? When we think about saving time for a moment we realize that in reality it is impossible to actually *save* time. Time will pass regardless of what we do.

What we can do, however, is to use time more effectively to achieve our goals. That is what time management really is. Have you ever heard of the 80/20 rule regarding time management? It is an old concept and is stated simply: Eighty percent of our accomplishments result from 20 percent of our efforts. What constitutes that major part of our time that produces only 20 percent of our achievements? Mostly it is made up of the easy tasks that are time-consuming but not very productive, such as writing superfluous reports, filing and refiling, updating address books, looking for misplaced items, long-winded phone conversations, wading through nonessential mail, and a myriad of time-sponging activities that produce little, or do not directly lead toward achieving a goal.

The highly productive 20 percent of the work day consists of tasks that may be difficult, risky (not necessarily physically), unpleasant, or otherwise more challenging.

Observing the operation of your business more closely, praising deserving subordinates, keeping in touch with future needs and directions, and making decisions are examples of actions that create results.

To help reduce low productivity, you might practice a form of what is called, in emergency medicine, triage. Triage means you assign a priority for attention. The injured who have little chance to survive even with much attention are last to be treated; those minimally injured who can wait for treatment are next to last; and the group of injured who need immediate attention and have a good chance of survival are first to be treated. While this may seem cruel or insensitive, such a priority ranking is essential for the most lives to be saved with limited resources in emergency medicine or battle conditions.

In much the same way, you can triage your daily, weekly, and even monthly activities. Those actions or situations that most directly influence the achievement of your goals receive your first attention; those that have some bearing on your goal achievement are next; and those that have little or no relation to your objectives receive the time left over. Even your daily mail can be sorted and acted upon based on such a ranking.

If you implement and stay with a priority system you will be surprised at how much more efficiently you use your time and how much more quickly you realize your goals. Time is the one commodity that cannot be bought, stretched, saved, or reused. Use it wisely and with forethought.

New workaholics have a bias toward action. When your goals are clear and specific, then you will also have the basis for an action plan to accomplish them. As Norman Mailer has said, "It is actions not sentiments which make history." Effective use of time allows you to get more accomplished with better end results.

3

Innovators and Superstars

*N*ow that we have outlined the 10 characteristics of the new workaholic, it would be easy to believe that an individual is born to be a new workaholic just as it is easy to believe that Beethoven was born with his ability to play and compose music. If you believe all new workaholics are born, then you have bought into a myth, an untruth that persists in the face of scientific evidence to the contrary.

Charles Garfield reported on a 1980 study of world-class Soviet athletes. Four groups were tested. The group that received the most intensive mental training showed the greatest improvement, while the group that used only physical training showed the least. Those results can be directly extrapolated to individuals in business and other professions. What we have drawn from the training of athletes is that high-level performance can be learned and the imagery and mental rehearsal are effective adjunctive training to physical practice.

Over the past 20 years Western society has learned from research conducted by the Soviets and East Germans that it is not merely a select few who can develop into high-level performers. Nearly anyone can if they apply specific, learned techniques diligently and repeatedly.

This growing body of evidence suggests that we may no longer legitimately argue for our inherited limitations. The other implication of the research is that improving performance is not an all-or-nothing endeavor, and to reap the rewards of being a high-level performer, you can pick and choose what characteristics you wish to develop more fully.

We will provide you with a practical program for developing each of the 10 traits we mentioned earlier. In our workshops we personalize the techniques for the specific situations and individuals in an organization, and in this book we offer as many different examples as possible. This will allow you to test a variety of situations and adapt the techniques to your own particular set of circumstances, goals, weaknesses, and strengths.

In our work we have found there are five general categories of skills and strategies that apply toward achievement of optimal performance. Each category has subgroups. They are listed in this manner:

The Hyper-Performer's Success Formula

I. Executive superskills—the A.I.M. Strategy for Mental Fitness™
   1. (A) Active relaxation
   2. (I) Imagery of the end result
   3. (M) Mental rehearsal

II. Cognitive strategies
   1. Behavior modification/feedback
   2. Self-talk; affirmations; feed forward
   3. Relationship skills
   4. Worst-case scenario
   5. Advantage/disadvantage list
   6. Systematic desensitization
   7. Communication skills
   8. Goal setting
   9. Cues
   10. Assertiveness training
   11. Role playing
   12. Journal writing

13. Psychotherapy/counseling
14. Time management skills
15. Creativity training

III. Strategic lifestyle management
1. Stress management
2. Sleep
3. Leisure time
4. Nutrition
5. Exercise
6. Habit control; alcohol/tobacco/drugs
7. Yoga/meditation/martial arts training
8. Physical appearance
9. Physical checkups

IV. Knowledge
1. Books/audiotapes/videotapes
2. Workshops/seminars
3. Magazines/journals
4. Brainstorming
5. Memory training
6. Professional conferences/meetings
7. Networking
8. Computer databases
9. Informal discussion groups
10. Coaches/counselors/mentors

V. Miscellaneous
1. Role models: mentors/biographies/peers/family/ friends
2. Humor
3. Support groups

If an individual desires to become an optimal performer, he or she should be able to utilize the various categories and subgroups above to develop the 10 characteristics we described earlier. In fact, we have found that each of the 10 traits have specific strategies that seem to work best. Through observation and testing we have found the following categories and subgroups to be of most value in developing each of the traits.

Hyper-Performance Strategies

When you have determined which characteristics you wish to develop, study the formulas below, which show you which strategies are most effective. For example, if you plan to enhance your passion and enthusiasm toward your career, you would look back to the Hyper-Performance Success Formula above and find that you can apply: I—all of the Executive superskills; II 2—the cognitive strategy of self-talk, affirmations, and feed forward, which is similar to feedback except that you are using mental rehearsal to imagine positive responses in future situations; III 1–7—the strategic lifestyle tactics of stress management to yoga; and finally V 1—imagery of yourself possessing the traits of mentors or others whom you respect.

These strategies can be used both in a conscious day-to-day application or as part of your mental rehearsal and imagery, which will be discussed later. The value of this formula is that you now have tangible avenues for improving any of the 10 optimal performance traits.

Characteristic	Strategy & Subgroup
1. Passion	I; II 2; III 1–7; V 1
2. Adaptability	I; II 2,4,5; III; IV 1–3,5,8; V 2,3
3. Present-Centered	I; II 7; III 1,8
4. Resourceful	I; II 3,10; IV; V 1,3

Characteristic	Strategy & Subgroup
5. Personal Power	I; II 1,2,8,11; IV; V 1,3
6. Perseverance	I; II 1,2; III 1,2; V 1,3
7. Optimism	I; II 1,2,9,11; III 1–7; V 1,2,3
8. Creativity	I; II 1,2,6,10; III 1; IV; V 2,3
9. Goal Setting	I; II 1,10; V 3
10. Time Management	I; II 10; V 3

Category I (the Superskills), with all three subgroups—active relaxation, imagery of the end result, and mental rehearsal—is the only one to appear in all the improvement strategies. We believe the Superskills are the most important strategies of all. Those skills can enhance every trait, without exception. They are the most powerful techniques one can practice because they work to enhance the effects of all the rest.

New Workaholics and Their Personal Lives

It has been a stereotype that success and devotion to work automatically mean a deterioration of personal life. While that is undeniably true for some executives, it is not a requirement for professional achievement. We believe that new workaholics can and do generally maintain an enjoyable personal and family life.

In research conducted by Professors Fernando Bartolome and Paul Evans and reported in the *Harvard Business Review,* the private and professional lives of over 2000 managers and their families was studied over a five-year span, and an interesting factor was discovered. Two groups of executives were identified, one whose private lives deteriorated, and one whose private lives were well functioning and happy. The difference between the two groups was not a function of how much they worked (both groups worked hard and intently). Rather, the difference was negative emotional spillover.

Bartolome and Evans found that managers who were unhappy in their work had a limited chance of enjoying happiness at home, regardless of how little they traveled, or how much they vacationed or spent time at home. When managers were happy at work, a positive emotional spillover led to more happiness at home. So it was not work, travel, or time away from family that determined enjoyable personal lives. It was the degree of emotional satisfaction and happiness in their work that was the determining factor.

Because we know that excessive stress leads to emotional and physical turmoil, an excellent starting point for creating more happiness and satisfaction in one's work is to dissolve excessive stress through a program of active relaxation. Active relaxation can be accomplished in many ways; however, you should set aside a specific amount of time *each day* (about 10 to 20 minutes) for this activity.

The active relaxation process begins with your selective concentration while you are fully awake. You may focus on an object, a part of your body, a word, or even a mental image of an object. As you focus, you take slow, deep breaths and hold the breath for several counts before exhaling.

When you concentrate on relaxing, developing an active mental relaxation process, you also initiate biochemical changes in your body. Individuals have been monitored to measure brain activity, heart rate, blood pressure, muscle tension, galvanic skin resistance, metabolism, and a number of other involuntary, biological functions. Active relaxation affects these functions in an opposite manner to the stress response mentioned earlier. This relaxation response is the body's way of countering the negative effects of stress.

The wonderful side effect of this stress reduction is that those same relaxation responses are part of the Superskills, which lead to optimal performance. Active relaxation is the setup or foundation for end-result imagery and mental rehearsal. Imagery of the end objective and mental rehearsal are what great athletes use. People often use mental rehearsal without realizing that is what they are practicing.

For instance, mental rehearsal is the imaging of an action or event process. To some people, imaging means to visualize; however, visualization is only one form of imaging. Imaging encompasses all the senses. Seeing, smelling, feeling, tasting, hearing, and even emotions can be imaged and rehearsed in our minds. Winning athletes use imagery to rehearse their performance before every critical action.

An example is Dick Fosberry, the world champion high jumper who said of the 1968 Olympic event in Mexico City that he spent time before each jump visualizing every part of his upcoming jump. He knew he was ready when he imagined himself successfully clearing the bar.

Jack Nicklaus uses end-result imagery unfailingly, and in combination with process imagery. He comments, "Visualizing the swing is useless if you fail to visualize what it is supposed to achieve."

The combination of end-result imagery and mental rehearsal, along with regular physical practice, has produced many world-class winners. Studies show clearly that our minds and bodies cannot tell the difference between an event imagined and one that physically took place. When you imagine an action, your brain sends action potentials— motor electrical currents—to the exact muscles used in that event. In essence you mentally perform that physical action.

There is a special kind of learning process that takes place in the brain during mental rehearsal. As you practice an action, maneuver, or any task, your brain records the patterns in what are called engrams. Engrams are believed to be imprints created in the brain that allow for nearly automatic replays of those practiced patterns. When a basketball player, for example, practices free-throws he or she develops engrams or a brain record of the angle, velocity, and other data necessary to sink the ball.

As more success is developed the engrams become more accurate and eventually the free-throw becomes nearly automatic, with little concern for the physical process involved: holding the ball, balance of the body, hands and ball up over the head, and so on. It all flows in one smooth action. You need only concentrate to allow those engrams to control the muscles.

Many research studies demonstrate that this patterning, or engram process, is evoked even when the event is imagined. The value of imagery and mental rehearsal is in creating engrams of successful completion. Your unconscious will work toward accomplishing your goals while your brain is patterning engrams for accomplishing the action processes necessary to be successful.

Even though the exact process by which the unconscious creates the proper engrams is not yet understood, we know that it works, so we use it.

Additionally, end-result imagery is not an all-or-nothing process. Even if you are not practicing it at its most potent level, it can still be effective.

How can this be applied to a specific business application? In taking the Personal Inventory Profile™ for the 10 new workaholic traits, you will identify weak traits as well as those in which you are already strong. However, even if you practice active relaxation and imagery less than diligently, you will still experience some change.

Relating the Superskills to a Practical Business Application

Throughout our lives we are engaged in negotiation; for career moves, in personal relationships, as a consumer, and often in our work. Even routine negotiations that many people consider to be transactions, such as returning a pair of shoes because of a defect, are arenas of negotiation. But here is an example of improving the outcome of negotiations and how one client of ours utilized the A.I.M. strategy to sharpen his negotiating skills.

Howard is a real estate developer specializing in commercial property. He regularly must negotiate with banking institutions and private investment groups for financing of projects. He devotes 15 to 20 minutes each day, usually in the morning after he arrives at the office and before he begins his daily work, to active relaxation and imagery.

He only needs about 10 minutes of active relaxation to become very relaxed and ready for his imagery and mental rehearsal because of his familiarity with the relaxation skill. To sharpen his negotiating skills, he images the building he wants to construct as being already built and occupied with paying tenants.

One of the principles Howard has in his business is that he is more concerned with having a profitable development take place than in how it comes about. So his mental rehearsal involves an array of possibilities, all of which can lead to a successful agreement. Specifically, he imagines that regardless of what opposition he will be negotiating against, he will probe until he discovers the point upon which he can create a profitable outcome. Where others might set their sights on specific interest rates, points, or payment schedules, Howard imagines himself as having many options open to him, much as a building may have many openings.

Additionally, he mentally rehearses how relaxed he will be at a meeting, and how inventive he can be in seeing possibilities that may not be obvious. He rehearses by focusing on the words, inflections, gestures, and other subtle indicators in his negotiation.

Howard consciously selects useful material for his imagery and mental rehearsal throughout his day and jots down a sentence or a few key words as reminders. When he practices his imagery for those few minutes each day, he often has new material that relates closely to his current situations. For example, during the time he was negotiating for a zoning variance on a piece of property, his car overheated and he had to replace the radiator. In his mental rehearsal the next day he imagined himself being cool as a new radiator even in the presence of a long uphill climb over the frustrations of dealing with a government agency.

That image, and others like it, taken from his immediate environment helped him through the long process required to obtain the needed variance. The most effective imagery includes familiar material. With a little forethought you will soon be able to find a great deal of material in your day-to-day life that can be adapted to your imagery objectives and mental rehearsal. Keep a notebook or tape recorder handy to make notes of exceptionally good material, as Howard does.

Type A and B Personalities and New Workaholics

There has been a great deal written about Type A and Type B personalities and how they relate to illness, performance, and personality characteristics. In *Type A Behavior and Your Heart*, Meyer Friedman and Ray Rosenman describe how personality patterns relate to causing and predicting heart disease. While heredity, diet, and abuses such as smoking and alcohol also influence susceptibility to illness, personality and behavior patterns were shown to have a major correlation to heart disease.

In a study of 3500 men (over 35 and under 60 years old) spanning a 10-year period, cardiologists Friedman and Rosenman found Type A men had three times the number of coronary conditions than Type B men. Their conclusion: "In the absence of Type A behavior pattern, coronary heart disease almost never occurs before 70 years of age, regardless of the fatty foods eaten, the cigarettes smoked, or the lack of exercise. But, when this behavior pattern is present, coronary heart disease can easily erupt in the thirties or forties."

Essentially, Type A traits induce and perpetuate the flight or fight response, and as that condition continues, a series of biological actions takes place. When the flight or fight response is triggered, an increased level of blood cholesterol develops due to an excessive amount of cathecholamines (the heart stimulating chemicals created when the body is over stressed). This causes a decrease in the clearing of blood

77

cholesterol and a tendency for the platelets and fibrinogen (blood clotting elements) to settle onto the walls of the veins and arteries. Eventually, the heart must work harder to circulate blood through the narrowing arteries. If even a small clot forms, it can lodge in one of the narrowing blood passages to the heart and a heart attack occurs.

From their studies, Friedman and Rosenman estimated that up to 50 percent of the U.S. population are Type A and 40 percent are Type B, and about 10 percent are a blend of the two.

Recent studies indicate that some of these earlier notions held about these Type A and B individuals may be incomplete. Howard Friedman, Judith Hall, and Monica Harris, in their study of Type A behavior, health, and style of expression, found subgroups of the two basic personality groups.

Two groups of Type A people were found in their study. One group was tense, repressed, and illness-prone (SOPs); while the other group was healthy, talkative, personable, and in control (hyper-performers). Within the two groups of Type B individuals was the first: healthy, easygoing, quiet types. A second subgroup of Type B was found whose personalities were submissive, repressed, tense, and possessing an external locus of control. They were often illness-prone (also SOPs).

Innovators and Superstars

Recent findings such as the one described above and by Gayle Privette of the University of West Florida, support what we have found in our work; there is a subgroup of Type A individuals who possess energy and application to their work, are charismatic, sociable, expressive, dominant, and are in control and coping well with the stresses in their lives.

Most innovators are new workaholics. Classic Type B people and Type B SOPs do not take many risks, and risk is necessary to be an innovator—the willingness to try and even fail occasionally to achieve what others may only dream about. New workaholics are easy to spot in an organization. They are usually recognized as superstars by their superiors, and are the consistent high achievers.

Type A SOPs may exhibit some innovation and occasional bursts of risk and achievement, but over a period of time they will also exhibit the negative characteristics of hostility, anger, competitiveness, and the resultant erratic performance.

The previous concept of Type A personalities formulated by Friedman and Rosenman in 1974 described a person who was aggressively involved in a chronic struggle to achieve more and more in less and less time. This description was expanded to emotional, as well as physical, characteristics. The person walks briskly, has an alert face and eyes, a jaw-grinding facial set, accelerating speech with few pauses midsentence, a firm handshake, and an explosive temperament.

What sets this newly recognized group of classic Type A SOPs apart from the subgroup that are new workaholics, is that SOPs are impatient, hostile, tense, and lack or perceive a lack of control over their lives. The SOPs are the people who were considered to be workaholics in the past. Individuals who possessed drive, intensity, and control and were devoid of hostility were considered to be Type B by default. Indeed, there are also individuals who might be categorized as Type B personalities who are relaxed, quiet, nonexpressive, methodical, and not illness prone, and who are potential new workaholics. They can develop the specific traits needed to become new workaholics.

Classic Type B individuals will seldom desire to become

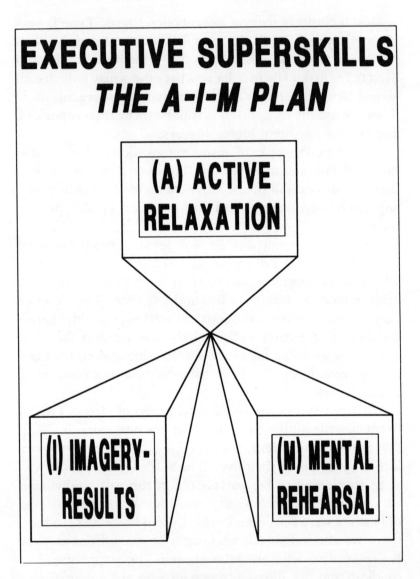

FIGURE 4.

hyper-performers. Wise CEOs recognize the assets Type B people bring to an organization. Leaders should utilize them for their strengths rather than try, often futilely, to make them over into Type A new workaholics. Classic Type B individuals are usually happy where they are in life, and make fine administrators and organizational employees.

New Workaholics Are Made, Not Born

As you read about new workaholics you might wonder how individuals become new workaholics, whether they develop in childhood, learn from experience, or have a sudden revelation that transforms them. The unsatisfying answer is that individuals become new workaholics by all those paths. In some situations children learn a specific set of values from their parents and those values become translated into hyper-performance in adulthood. For others, the characteristics come from personality developments outside the home. And it seems that other people refine their present skills with focus and purpose.

Consider the case of a colleague who became a new workaholic. Richard is a physician who has been in practice for many years, and by many measures is successful.

Relative to most professionals, Richard was successful rather quickly, as is possible in medicine. However, he was not very happy. He enjoyed going to work, but he had few outside interests and was not, by his own description, much fun to be around. In time he became bored with his practice and though he was not prone to alcohol or drug abuse, he could easily have drifted into some form of harmful addiction, which he felt might have been food.

Richard would come home after work and eat a big meal, sit and read a professional journal, or turn on the television and tune out his family and most of the rest of the world. He was gradually alienating his family through indifference, and he was isolating himself from acquaintances and friends. It was getting more severe each month. Later his wife told him that had a change in their relationship not occurred, she believed their marriage would not have survived.

The catalyst for change came one day when a former college buddy of Richard's, and perhaps his only remaining friend, collapsed and died while routinely jogging. Richard's friend was on the eve of his 44th birthday, just 3 years older than Richard at that time. It was the suddenness of his friend's death that shook Richard into a self-evaluation.

Richard's friend did have one big risk factor—he was a classic Type A, not the new Type A subgroup personality. Richard found, in his self-assessment, that he also had some of those dangerous Type A characteristics. That discovery scared him enough to want to change.

Until individuals recognize the need to make some alterations in their life, the rut will likely get deeper before they will find a path out of it.

Turtles and Race Horses

We recognize that many top CEOs who are reading this book may already have developed the 10 characteristics of high-level performers we describe. Those CEOs may want to help their key subordinates and managers gravitate toward becoming new workaholics.

A top executive can best work with SOPs who exhibit good motivation and a desire to become high-level performers and help them become new workaholics.

Hans Selye related his view of personality types to a turtle and a race horse. The turtle is the classic Type B—healthy, perseverant, and noncompetitive—while the race horse is the new workaholic. When a turtle tries to be a racehorse, the turtle may become a classic Type A, or Type B SOP, with all the incipient problems of stress and illness. With the A.I.M. Program we present here, there is a good likelihood that the motivated SOP can develop some of the characteristics of a new workaholic.

On the other hand, if race horses try to become turtles, they may become unhealthy Type B SOPs, over-controlled inhibitors who have traded one occupational side effect for another. It is important to not push subordinates or yourself into a role that is neither comfortable nor satisfying. If you take a new workaholic who is functioning well but who believes that he or she is prone to heart problems, and wants to be a Type B, that individual might very well end up becoming an unhealthy, over-controlled B who would be frustrated at the slower pace. Such a transformation, if it were possible, would spell unhappiness. That individual would do better by striving to become a more relaxed, less stressed new workaholic and enjoy that accomplishment.

An excellent way to begin such an in-house improvement program is to assess your present situation and also decide which personnel are motivated to become more efficient and also desire to perform closer to their potential and enhance their health. Then design a strategy to further motivate these individuals and provide them with a realistic program for achieving their professional goals and objectives. However, even if you are a classic Type B personality this book will help you understand new workaholics with whom you may work.

Privette developed a model for peak experience and peak performance, which also correlates closely to our studies of new workaholics. She found that as individuals have peak experiences (those she describes as ecstasy or extreme happiness) they develop what has been called a flow state.

The term flow state was first coined by Mihaly Csikszentmihalyi. The nature of the flow state is one of rapt attention and ultraconcentration. It can occur during artistic activities, during sports or other physical activity, while in an intellectual engagement such as chess, or at work, and most certainly while at play. In fact, Csikszentmihalyi believes that all those activities and many more can be experiential states that are forms of play.

Psychologists usually focus on play as a form of therapy or as some means to an end, but seldom as a process to understand for its own sake. Philosophers from Plato to Sartre have noted that individuals are most human, creative, free, and complete when they play. Play is a relatively spontaneous human act during which we are free of our basic needs and duties. Put simply, play is fun.

What Csikszentmihalyi found in his interviews and questionnaires of dancers, chess players, athletes, musicians, surgeons, teachers, and rock climbers was that while in flow, they experienced sensations of total involvement. That total absorption, much like a child at play who fails to hear an outside voice calling, is the unified experience of the self and the environment of the play activity. Though not all play is flow, he additionally believes that the flow experience is dependent on flow activities. We experience the state as a unified movement from one moment to the next, one action flowing to another based on an internal logic. We feel in control of our actions, yet we seem to need no conscious intervention to maintain the flow.

The flow state can be accessed almost inadvertently through a centering of attention. An example is Jimmy, who went to a night club for the first time. He asked a girl to dance; it was one of the few times he'd ever danced with a girl. Even though he was not very adept, he was so entranced with his partner that he entered a flow state and danced with the girl as if they had danced together for years. For the entire time of that flow state he was oblivious to all his surroundings except for the girl.

Another example of a flow state is that of a young man working with a friend in a small restaurant that was noted for its excellent ice cream. In the evening from seven to midnight they were responsible for all orders, both takeout and on premises, everything from ice cream to sandwiches.

For four hours the two of them worked with such an economy of motion and so fluidly that not once did they collide or stumble around each other. One of the young men described the four hours as a sort of fantasy time in which he could do no wrong.

Even in their flurry of motion and abrupt turns and moves their motions blended so that they must have appeared, if someone were watching with intent, to be one unit, though separate beings. Such a flow state can also be found in more sophisticated situations, in creative situations such as the arts. But the flow states experienced by engineers, programmers, speakers, business executives, and athletes are just as valuable.

The flow state is closely related to play but is not exclusive to it. What Maslow has called peak experiences and what some call religious rapture share many distinctive features with the flow process. Certainly we believe that the flow state can also occur during work and the peak experiences or flow states that Privette describes may be felt, for example, by an executive during a brainstorming session.

This is how one executive we spoke to described his flow state. "I am unaware of the traffic outside the building or of the muffled sound of phones in another room. I'm imagining a new idea and the factors that will play on it. I may be doodling on paper the costs, the time involvement, even the possible marketing strategies, and the doors of possibilities seem to open merely by approaching them. It's as though I don't want to stop that process because the idea might suddenly get clobbered by some future event that's out of my control."

We have found that active relaxation and imagery create a fertile ground for developing flow states. When an individual is engaged in work that she or he enjoys, it takes on the same characteristics as play. That playful state of mind can be imagined and that imagination creates the same successful engram patterns in the brain as if one had actually experienced a flow state. Of course, this sort of imagined flow state may not be achieved every time, and it is not necessary for the imagery to be perfect in order to be effective.

This experience of flow is accessible to the new workaholic, but seldom to the SOP. It is that combination of peak experience and optimal performance that the new workaholic strives to attain.

So, it is Type A individuals with control and without hostility, who are happy at their work and who can use the flow state to develop their optimal performance levels. And it is the A.I.M. program that can help create and channel the flow state to sharpen those traits and move an individual toward becoming a new workaholic.

Internally motivated, Type A individuals who have low self-esteem and who are hostile, competitive, generally unhappy, threatened, and illness-prone may use the A.I.M. plan to move themselves toward peak experience and high-level performance. Often these employees can be channeled toward being new workaholics when given the skills. A personal teaching experience of these new workaholic skills is most effective because these Type A SOPs may be resistant to indirect suggestions for change. The very nature of their hostility and defensiveness may prevent them from taking the steps necessary to change their direction toward successful patterns for themselves and their firm.

Almost all new workaholics will be a subgroup of Type A; however, not all Type As are new workaholics. Conversely, not all SOPs are Type A, and SOPs can be Type B personalities also.

In all this discussion of Type A and Type B personalities the most relevant features to the new workaholism are control and coping. The individuals in both personality type subgroups who exhibit control, lack hostility, and possess stress coping mechanisms are highly likely to be or become new workaholics. The SOPs are not high-level performers and are illness-prone, while the new workaholic is an optimal performer and is not illness-prone.

It is also important to recognize that occasionally SOPs may produce high-level performance. The difference is, however, that they will not be able to sustain that level. In order to sustain high levels of achievement you must find enjoyment and a sense of peak experience or flow, as Privette discovered. It is that positive reinforcement of the experience that allows you to keep up that pace. Only if you like what you are doing can you sustain it. The SOPs are riddled with the bullets of stress and held back by the weight of hostility and lack of control. It is the anxiety and energy of their personality that masquerades as new workaholism.

We are not advocating peak performance. That is like a mountain top; there are deep valleys between the peaks. You may only reach peaks once in a while. New workaholics strive for optimal performance; sustained high-level achievement. And you have to feel good about achieving it to maintain that level.

What we mean by sustained high levels of performance is relative. Many hyper-performers have sustained high levels in certain characteristics, but may not achieve the highest levels in other traits. For example, an executive may have achieved optimal levels of performance in 8 of the 10 traits, but still lack sustained achievement in optimism and adaptability. The short-fall in those two areas may prevent the executive from achieving his or her full potential. The Superskills can be useful in elevating the performance in those specific areas while maintaining it in the other areas.

The A.I.M. program can be trait specific. But active relaxation, imagery of your goal, and mental rehearsal have the beneficial side effect of being a stress-coping mechanism and enhancing all the other positive characteristics at the same time. It is particularly active relaxation that neutralizes excessive stress. No other skills have such far-reaching positive effects. Stress in the SOP is the single most inhibiting factor to high-level performance and achievement. Active relaxation allows new workaholics to utilize their imagery for positive gains and to prevent stress-related illness.

The process of active relaxation is easy to learn, and the benefits are immediate and far-reaching. In the next chapter we will show you how to practice active relaxation and what you can expect to feel from it.

4

Neanderthals Never
Used Freeways

*N*eanderthals never used freeways or they would likely have been plagued by many of the same stress related illnesses we have in our present society. We inherited our fight or flight reaction from our primitive ancestors who were more worried about sabre-toothed tigers and dinosaurs than adjustable rate mortgages and traffic snarls on the way to work. Fortunately for them, the tiger or tyrannosaurus was either fought or fled from, and the biochemical responses to those threatening situations usually subsided within a few hours.

Unfortunately for us, the stresses and response-producing conditions that we face in present society are not so quickly dealt with. The mounting stresses that confront us linger; seldom can we run from them easily. Sooner or later the symptoms of excessive, harmful stress will develop in one form or another and if not heeded, more serious results may follow.

David has been feeling anxious and pressured for nearly a year and knows that he needs to do something about it. He enrolled in a health club and went several times a week for about two months, but found other obligations superseded his workouts. His doctor suggested self-hypnosis for relaxation, so David read a book and did some deep breathing and relaxation for a few weeks, but he lost the momentum when he left town for a week on business. He has been experiencing chronic indigestion for over two months and his doctor believes he is heading for an ulcer. David takes antacids, avoids spicy foods, and believes a vacation will head off an ulcer.

The reaction of many people to the symptoms of stress in their lives is to treat the symptoms. If the symptoms go away they believe the cause did, too. In our society we cannot afford the false security of the Ostrich Effect—putting our consciousness in the sand and ignoring the stress in our lives. The physical, emotional, and psychological effects of excessive stress cannot be dodged by ignoring them or escaped by good intentions to deal with them later.

The corrosiveness of stress cannot be ducked with Maalox and five days in Jamaica. If the stress-causing situations persist, you need an ongoing method of neutralizing them. Relaxation is a generality. It can mean anything from going to a movie to taking Valium. While active relaxation is a specific technique and requires learning a skill, it is one of the best long-term techniques for effectively dealing with day-to-day stress.

Active relaxation promotes good health and is an excellent stress management and stress coping technique. It is also the pathway to developing effective imagery and mental rehearsal to enhance any of the 10 high-level characteristics we have discussed. In this chapter we will show you how these strategies work and how you can apply them to specific objectives.

A typical example is Rita, a 34-year old sales manager in a cosmetics manufacturing firm. Rita is a single parent, and has an ailing mother. Six representatives in her region report to her, and she is responsible for meeting quarterly sales objectives. Her sales force has rugged competition, and she is searching for a new promotion tactic to achieve her sales goals.

Every Thursday she meets with her general sales manager to discuss her progress and plans. If she believes she is likely to fall short of her sales target at the end of each quarter, she feels the increasing pressure at the Thursday meetings. She is doing the best she can but still has a nagging sense of disappointment.

Add to these career pressures the responsibilities of raising a 7-year-old son and concern over her mother's congestive heart failure. It is clear that Rita is under an ongoing, multilayered set of stress-causing conditions that our primitive ancestors never encountered. Fortunately, Rita's company understands the need for stress coping methods and has provided all of their management people with workshops teaching stress management skills.

She exercises regularly, sets aside 25 minutes every day for private relaxation time, and goes out dancing with friends once a week. She is not ignorant of her need to dissipate the tension buildup in her life. Rita handles her life successfully. Success for Rita is measured by more than dollars. She derives a feeling of gratification from her work and her son. Rita's friends tell her they can see the personal growth in her.

Research shows that our bodies and minds are deeply connected. As we focus on and develop one component of the relaxation response within us the other components are also initiated. Herbert Benson described the relaxation response as the opposite of the fight or flight response—the opposite of stress. The relaxation response is characterized by:

1. Deeper and slower breathing
2. Slower heart rate
3. Increased blood flow to the extremities
4. Lower muscle tension
5. Lower metabolism
6. More balanced hormonal activity
7. Lower blood pressure

What Benson found in his research was that initiating any one of these characteristics will induce the others to follow. While most of these features of the relaxation response are under control by our autonomic nervous system, our breathing is controllable by our conscious mind. When we deliberately breathe deeply and slowly from the diaphragm, we start a chain of internal responses that lead to a quiet, balanced, relaxed state.

It has become clear in innumerable studies that our bodies and minds are deeply connected. Norman Cousins presents a well documented case for this duality from his own personal health experiences. In his book *The Healing Heart,* he explores the link between his heart condition and his high stress levels.

Cousins chronicles the connection of lower stress and his return to health. He comments, "Certainly, emotional and psychological factors, which figure so largely in bringing about heart disease, are vital to any recovery program."

Friedman and Rosenman, in their studies of Type A and Type B personalities, found that the cholesterol levels of accountants shot up as federal income tax deadlines drew close. The same was found of medical students just before final exams.

The cost of stress to American business may be incalculable, but it is certainly enormous. In fact, recent court cases have allowed worker's compensation for stress-related claims. In California alone the number of mental-stress injury claims reported to the worker's comp board more than tripled, from 1282 in 1980 to 4236 in 1984. According to the National Council on Compensation Insurance, the stress claims not related to physical injury first appeared in the late 1970s, accounting for only 2.5 percent of claims, but by 1983 the figure was 14.9 percent.

Without a stress management program for employees,

many large companies are noticing not only more worker's compensation claims, but also absenteeism and lower productivity. Effective stress control can mitigate these losses.

There are many ways to initiate the relaxation response. Certainly, meditation, biofeedback, yoga, self-hypnosis, deep breathing, and other methods are effective. However, one of the easiest, most versatile, and most complete method of relaxation is active progressive relaxation.

The power of this mind/body connection is simple to utilize through the language of mind—imagery. It is imagery through which we can focus on and elicit any part of the relaxation response and thereby tip the first domino of the relaxation response.

The Active Relaxation Technique

Active relaxation was introduced by Edmund Jacobson in a form he called active progressive relaxation. Though there are many variations, we will provide you with the one we use most frequently and that we believe is the easiest to learn and the most effective.

Though you will soon be able to practice active relaxation almost anywhere, in the beginning we suggest you find a quiet, comfortable place where you will not be disturbed for 20 to 30 minutes. A place where you may sit or lie comfortably with subdued light is best. Have your calls held or disconnect the phone if you can.

Many organizations have set aside time-out rooms, where audio and video facilities allow employees to listen to relaxation, goal-setting, motivational, or other tapes privately with earphones. Time-out rooms also allow for uninterrupted segments of 10 to 20 minutes for active relaxation and imagery practice.

A study conducted by Ruanne Peters, Herbert Benson, and Douglas Porter on the effects of daily relaxation-response breaks in working environments showed positive evidence of the effectiveness of such relaxation on health, performance, and well being. In a 12-week study it was found that the group that was taught and that practiced relaxation exercises daily reported significant improvements in physical and emotional symptoms, illness days off, performance, and general happiness over two control groups. One control group was instructed to sit quietly for two 15-minute relaxation breaks, and the other group received no breaks and no instructions whatsoever.

It was found that even with less than daily practice some improvements were noticed. Peters, Benson, and Porter found that the workplace is an ideal setting for stress prevention programs because most managers and executives spend at least half their waking hours at work. If brief periods of time are taken throughout the workday, increased performance is the result. Again we see that harm to SOPs comes not from an inability to be consistent with the A.I.M. program, but rather from not doing it at all.

You may wish to practice a relaxation experience right now. Or you may wish to make a tape of the following guide to active relaxation and play it during the time you set aside each day for active relaxation. We believe that audio tapes can be useful in learning and refining active relaxation, whether you create your own tapes or purchase some of the better tapes on the market.

An Active Relaxation Exercise

From your comfortable position find an object, a spot, or any visual focus in front of you and fix your concentration on that visual spot. The process of active relaxation is accelerated by your channeled concentration and limited visual distractions. As you focus on your spot visually, mentally concentrate on your slow, regular, deep breathing. Breathe in comfortably to a slow count of five, hold the breath for another count of five and then slowly release the air to a count of eight.

By holding the breath and releasing it slowly you prevent hyperventilation, so be conscious of your counting and do not take so deep a breath as to cause a burning or painful sensation in your chest or lungs. Diaphragmatic breathing is called stomach breathing, that is, as you inhale allow your stomach to bulge out. As your diaphragm stretches, your stomach distends, and though this may not appear very attractive to you, the nature of this type of deep breathing is much healthier than chest breathing.

The rib cage surrounding your lungs has a limited capacity for expansion. Expanding your chest to take breaths does not allow the depth that diaphragmatic breathing does. It is this sort of deep, slow, stomach-expanding breathing that begins the relaxation response. Your focused mental concentration on your breathing and your visual focus on the spot you've chosen eliminates conscious distractions and promotes the next phase of your active relaxation.

The next step in active relaxation is to systematically gather tension to each major part of your body and then deliberately release it. Becoming aware of the tension created in each muscle group gives you more control over the release of it. You may begin with any part of your body. However, for this illustration begin with your feet; extremities that take a lot of weight and abuse through the day are a good place to start releasing stress and tension.

Throughout active relaxation you may continue staring at the focus spot, or you may close your eyes and mentally picture the part of your body you are actively relaxing. Begin by imagining all the tension and stress in your legs moving down to your toes. As you imagine the tension flowing to your toes slowly tense the muscles in your feet by curling your toes downward and tightening the muscles. Continue your slow, deep breaths, and as you gather the tension in your feet over the span of two or three deep breaths take one more deep breath, hold that tension in your feet and then as you slowing exhale, simultaneously and slowly release the muscle tension in your feet. Repeat this process.

Next shift your concentration to your legs. As you continue

your deep breathing, imagine the stress and tension in your body flowing to your legs as you gradually tense the muscles in your thighs and calves. Build the muscle tension in your legs for two or three slow breaths and imagine all the stress and pressures from the day flowing down to your legs as the muscles become more and more tense and contracted. Take one more deep breath, hold it and then as you slowly release it, slowly relax your leg muscles and imagine all the stress and tension of the day being released at the same time. Repeat this process.

Next imagine the tension flowing to your groin and abdominal muscles. Take several deep breaths and slowly contract your buttocks, abdominal and groin muscles as you imagine the tension in your body, like sand in an hourglass, flowing into those muscles and becoming trapped there. After two or three breaths imagine the tension escaping from you as you release and relax those muscles. Repeat this procedure.

Take a deep breath and gradually tense your chest and back muscles. Imagine how your lungs can draw the stress and tension from all the parts of your body as you slowly breathe in and tense your back and chest muscles. Remember to breathe from your stomach, and even though it will be difficult to separately tense your chest muscles while allowing your abdominal muscles to expand with your breathing, do the best you can.

As you are breathing, imagine your stress being drawn into your lungs like dark smoke drawn into a balloon. Hold the tension there in your lungs for a few deep breaths, then take one more slow deep breath, hold it for a count of 10, then very slowly exhale and release the muscle tension at the same time. When you reach the end of your breath see if you can squeeze out just a little more air and a little more tension. Relax even more for a few moments and let your breathing continue to be slow and regular. After a few minutes, repeat this process.

By this point you will be noticeably more relaxed. However, you have a few more muscle groups to relax, and there is undoubtedly more tension stored that you have yet to release. But, it is valuable, particularly in the first few sessions of active relaxation, to pause at this point to recognize how much difference there is from the beginning to this level of relaxation. You might even evaluate what you believe your relaxation level presently is on a scale of 1 to 10. Make a mental note of your impressions at this point.

Next, clench both fists at the same time, and imagine grasping all the remaining tension in your body with those fists. Take a deep, satisfying, comfortable breath and gradually make your fists as tight as you can. Hold that muscle tension and let it build just a bit more if possible as you take one more deep breath and hold it. Then as you slowly exhale, release the tension in your fists and imagine letting go of all the tension and stress gathered there as you relax and open your fists.

Now, keeping your hands as relaxed as you can, take a deep breath and stiffen your arms and tighten your arm muscles as you concentrate on directing all the remaining tension in your body to your arms. Breathe deeply and hold your breath as you mentally gather the tension into your arms much like you might gather sticks in your arms for a campfire. Hold the tension and your breath for a count of 10 and then slowly exhale and slowly release the tension in your arms as you mentally imagine the sticks you were holding falling to the ground as your arms become loose and limp.

The next muscle group to focus on is your shoulders and neck. These are muscle groups that typically store a great deal of tension in many people. Be aware of how they feel just before you tense them. Then, take a deep breath and hunch your shoulders up as you tighten the muscles in your shoulders and neck. As you gradually tighten those muscles imagine all the weight of the day, all the pressures of the week loaded on your shoulders as you tighten and tense your shoulder and neck muscles. Imagine a backpack full of problems, worries, and tensions from the day pulling down on your shoulders as you resist with the muscle tension—image that as vividly as you can.

Take a deep breath, hold it for a count of 10, then as you slowly, deliberately exhale, imagine that backpack of tensions and worries breaking free and falling away from you. Take another deep breath and as you slowly exhale, imagine the backpack off your shoulders and on the ground; imagine the color of the backpack, the straps, the type of flap it might have and all the details you can.

Finally, focus on your face, forehead, and the muscles around your mouth. You use those muscles all day long for talking, for expressing your feelings, and for listening. These muscles perhaps more than any others are a reflection of your day's activities. Take a deep breath and slowly tighten all those muscles. Imagine your mouth open as if you were yelling loudly. Imagine your forehead deeply furrowed as while you are deep in thought. Imagine your eyes squinting as they might if you were intently gazing at a distant object on a sunny day.

Gather all the remaining tension in your body up into your head and face and as the muscles become tight and tense imagine your face as a mask that you can cast off. Take a deep breath, hold it for a count of 10 and slowly exhale as you relax all the muscles in your face and head. As you relax the muscles imagine that tight mask falling away and leaving your face relaxed and calm.

Now, take several regular, slow breaths and focus your attention on how relaxed you are. Move your head slowly from side to side, and perhaps rotate your shoulders just a bit.

Take a few more moments of slow regular breathing to recognize just how relaxed you are right now compared with before you began the relaxation session. Rate your present relaxation on a scale of 1 to 10, with 1 being the most relaxed. Do you notice a difference from what you felt a few minutes ago?

Place in your mental file the rating you put your relaxation at now so that you will remember how much difference there is after just 20 or 30 minutes of active relaxation. Appreciate what you have just done for yourself because it is a very healthy experience that will now lead you to many more positive experiences.

Notice any differences in your mood or thoughts. Be aware of any tingling in your hands or feet, or any sensation of warmth in your extremities or elsewhere. These are outward signs of physical changes that have come about as a result of your relaxation experience. They are positive indications that you can, indeed, bring about dramatic alterations in your physical and mental well-being.

For the first few sessions your goal may be to become as relaxed as you possibly can. As you repeat this process you will find that it takes you less and less time to reach the same level of relaxation. However, the essential thing is that you practice relaxation daily.

Remember that the A.I.M. program is not a trio of isolated events. Active relaxation, imagery of the end result, and mental rehearsal are powerful enlistments of your conscious, unconscious, and physical being to keep you healthy and your actions focused on your objectives.

5

Mental Fitness™ *and the Executive Superskills*

Over the past decade more and more Americans have been very concerned with keeping their bodies in good condition, for both cosmetic and health reasons. Certainly we endorse the health aspects of physical fitness and hope that it continues. At the same time, we have seen a great body of evidence that shows that mental conditioning can be effective in combatting the ill effects of stress—and stress, as we discussed earlier, can be linked to many serious illnesses that afflict us.

Through numerous studies conducted over the last few decades on athletes it has been shown that mental imagery provides a powerful boost to physical prowess, coordination, stamina, and preparedness. What has also been found more recently is that the same skills of end-result imagery and mental rehearsal are equally effective in enhancing almost any other activity we can engage in, including business and professional functions.

The two basic forms of imagery we have found most effective, and comprise the "I" and the "M" of the A.I.M. program, are end-result imagery and process imagery or mental rehearsal. End-result imagery was popularized by Maxwell Maltz in *Psycho-Cybernetics,* and consists of various mental images of your desired goal as having already taken place. Mental rehearsal, on the other hand, is made up of imagery of the actual or possible actions by which a desired objective could be accomplished.

Imagery and mental rehearsal have been demonstrated to have a positive influence on performance, and create bio-electrical responses in the human body. In the early 1930s

FIGURE 5. Type A and type B people who were tested for nonverbal expressiveness were divided into high or low categories. *Type A, high nonverbal expressiveness:* The healthy type A. The hyper-performer or new workaholic. This high powered performer is basically healthy and has a hardiness against the development of stress related diseases; *Type A, low nonverbal expressiveness:* The classical or unhealthy type A. It is what we call the type A SOP and what Dr. Friedman calls a hostile competitive; *Type B, low nonverbal expressiveness:* The classical healthy type B, or what we call the healthy nonworkaholic. Some may be high level performers but they *usually* do not reach the high levels of performance that the hyper-performer can achieve; *Type B, high nonverbal expressiveness:* A potentially unhealthy type B, a person who is not type B but is trying to be so. It is what we would call the type B SOP and what Dr. Friedman calls the over-controlled inhibitor.

Edmund Jacobson demonstrated that an individual's mental rehearsal of physical movements registered minute electrical stimulation of the exact muscles that would be used if the action had physically taken place. Other studies have provided evidence that imagery and mental rehearsal of a physical task, such as making free-throws with a basketball, can be just as effective and perhaps even more so, than actual physical practice. This is accomplished by daily, regular imagery of the task successfully completed. This is imagery of the end result—the basketball through the hoop.

We have found in our own work that hyper-performers—new workaholics—frequently use end-result imagery and mental rehearsal in their pursuit of high-level performance. The fundamental reason that imagery works is that you are planting a target that your unconscious mind will continually work toward.

Imagery in one form or another has been a technique used by many successful athletes. Jack Nicklaus believes that his game is 90 percent mental preparation, and he uses imagery as a part of that training. Nicklaus' description is a good example of imagery of the end result, and of the mental rehearsal of the process of achieving the end result. However, it is the imagery of the finished goal or objective that is the most powerful. "I never hit a shot, even in practice, without having a very sharp picture of it in my head first," Nicklaus says. He imagines the ball landing exactly where he wants it, and he pictures in his mind his stance, his putt, and the ball dropping nicely in the hole.

Arnold Schwarzenegger, the renowned body builder, used imagery as a significant part of his training programs.

The Soviets and the European sport community have been using imagery as part of their Olympic training for many years. The Swiss began using imagery training for their Olympic skiing team in 1968. They conducted a study of the physiologic changes between their skiers who actually trained on the giant slalom and those who only imagined their performance, and the effectiveness of both mental and physical training were the same. You can accomplish the same benefits of physical practice with mental imagery in far less time. When imagery is combined with actual practice the practice is cumulative.

The Swiss won three medals in 1968 and more in the 1972 Winter Olympics. The winner of three of those Olympic gold medals in skiing was Jean Claude Killy, who used imagery.

Imagery of the End Result

It is a common misconception that if we merely keep positive, goal-oriented thoughts consciously running through our mind our unconscious will process them as fact. Unfortunately, it is not quite that simple. In nearly everyone's mind there is what can be thought of as a control valve at the conscious level that allows some information received and processed to be fully accepted by the unconscious mind. The unconscious mind has no such control valve; it accepts all that it receives as fact and influences thought and physical process based upon those facts.

The storage capacity of the unconscious is virtually unlimited. Everything that we have ever perceived from any of our senses has been stored and is available to the unconscious mind even if we cannot consciously remember. It is that unquestioned acceptance by the unconscious that is our powerful ally in achieving our goals. However, we must bypass the conscious judgmental valve that prevents many of the positive affirmations and success oriented thoughts from reaching the unconscious mind.

Why would this internal judge of ours prevent wonderful, successful goals, images, and affirmations from reaching the unconscious? The answer is certainly different for each individual. However, there is often some fundamental disbelief or rejection of that positive information, due to what Denis Waitley, in his book *Seeds of Greatness,* calls F.E.A.R., or False Evidence Appearing Real. Often events or impressions from our childhood create fears, guilts, and misinformation upon which the conscious judge bases its decisions. Until something happens to remove or bypass those blockages, little of that positive information will reach the unconscious.

Imagery is considered to be the language of the unconscious, much as a computer operating system is the language of a computer. As Aristotle said, "The soul . . . never thinks without a picture." There has been much supporting evidence of this concept. One exciting description was developed by Karl Pribram, an eminent neuroscientist. He compares imagery with holography and describes how the essence of an original object is reproduced in a hologram. With much the same effect, imagery reproduces in the brain a replica of what the image represents. When the image is of an action, the brain and the unconscious mind do not seem to differentiate between the real and the imagined action. In this way, a mental picture can create the same bioelectrical brain responses as the physical action.

It is during the still moments of focus that those positive mental pictures are able to pass by the conscious control valve and move directly through to your unconscious mind. It has been found that when our conscious attention is focused on one thing very intently we are most ready to accept our own suggestions. It is as though the conscious judge is occupied with the object of your concentration while the intent of the image slips through to the unconscious. However, one or two whispers into the unconscious ear may not be enough to create a new priority or to cause the bioelectrical brain imprints to cause permanent change.

Once your goals become priorities, your unconscious begins to assist you in achieving your imagined objectives. Here is an analogy of one way the unconscious assists.

Think of your unconscious acceptance of your goals as a computer program that selectively stores and processes any and all information relevant to your goal. The program scans all new information available to it, and isolates and stores separately any information that can be used in making the best decisions and choices that advance you.

With this vast store of information, you will have available to your unconscious many more options and possibilities than your conscious mind alone would have had. The inclusion of that extra creative fodder is of most value when you mix and match that enormous store of information to develop new answers to problems, and perhaps new questions to be answered, which improves the decision-making process.

That is exactly what the human mind does day in and day out for most people. Imagery is one method of enlisting your unconscious mind to be a better computer than it already is.

For instance, if you were responsible for developing the next year's marketing strategy for your firm, you might use result imagery of how well you will feel after making a presentation to your board of directors, or chief executive officer. Image that presentation as having gone well; even though you may not yet have the words or the ideas that will compose your report you can imagine the positive results, including applause if that would be appropriate, and appreciation from your superiors. Your imagery can take on the aromas, the sounds of the surroundings, and incorporate responses from all of your senses.

For example, John is vice president of marketing for a large catalog merchandiser. It has been his five-year objective to start his own catalog company. He imagined himself as the owner in several different ways. He imagined the feeling of sitting behind a desk in his large office with catalog covers on the walls; he imagined signing on a bank account that bore his name, with the balance in the account in the millions of dollars.

He developed these images over a period of time, and he embellished each with more details and refinements. The desk became deep mahogany, with a high-back leather chair custom fit to his body. He imagined an unusual line of products for an upscale female market. At other times John imagined the successful rehearsal of key meetings with a corporation desiring to acquire his catalog company. He replayed his images routinely for three years. Recently he has begun his own business and has set his goals even higher.

Suppose you wished to use imagery for improving one of the 10 characteristics of a high-level achiever. For example, if enhanced time management was your objective you might imagine yourself leaving the office with your desk clear of all the important tasks for the day. Or, if your goal was increased perseverance, you could imagine yourself receiving an award for tenacity in solving a major project.

Determine before you practice your imagery what the signs of accomplishment for your objective will be. In the case of time management, the sign or signal marker might be 20 minutes time at the end of a day where everything is caught up and you have time to plan for tomorrow. And a real-life indicator of that perseverance could be making two more sales calls per day consistently for a month. Another benefit of setting progress signs for yourself is that you can include them in your imagery.

You might think of the unconscious mind as a supercomputer and your end-result imagery as instructions to change the programming. Your imagery is competing with all the other information and input, old and new, to your unconscious, which blends to create your conscious and unconscious behavior. Repetition of the end-result imagery is often needed to make your new objectives a priority.

Mental Rehearsal

The combination of end-result imagery and mental rehearsal can produce excellent results. For some applications, however, end-result imagery may not be as appropriate as mental rehearsal. Rehearsing the process by which you achieve your objective can have the benefit of helping to reduce tension and anxiety at the time of actual performance because of the familiarity with that process. Clinically, we talk of systematic desensitization; that is, you review the probable actions you will take, compartmentalize each element that may be troublesome, and gradually become less tense or fearful of the event or its outcome.

In selling situations, mental rehearsal can be very useful. For example, if you are going to make a selling presentation to a potential buyer and want to prepare for that meeting, the following process could help. Begin by imagining the setting you will be in, perhaps the buyer's office, a conference room, or if it will be a luncheon meeting, a restaurant.

Mentally rehearse how you will establish initial positive contact, asking an appropriate question about your prospect's vacation, the weather, a sports event, or other conversation starters that would be fitting for the situation. Then mentally picture recapping the past business contact you've had with that individual or others in that company so that you both have the same understanding of what has gone before this meeting. You might imagine some possible problems that may have occurred since your last contact and imagine how you would handle them.

Picture in your mind how you will begin your presentation, what the prospect's reactions might be, and how you would address them. Imagine as many objections as you can that might come up and how you would respond to each. In this sort of mental rehearsing you can create as difficult a presentation as you wish and imagine all the worst possibilities and how you would handle them.

If the presentation were important you would certainly be wise to arrange to rehearse as many times as possible beforehand, with at least three separate 10-minute rehearsal sessions. Such rehearsals as described above allow you to anticipate negative reactions and deal with them prior to the actual event, and help reduce anxiety and tension. You will be surprised to notice how much more effective you can be using this technique. When combined with repeated imagery of a sales presentation or other situation ending favorable, a powerful unconscious sequence of preparation takes place.

As you begin the A.I.M. Strategy it is best to devote 20 to 30 minutes a day to one particular objective you have. For that same goal you might develop four or five different images. One can blend into the next, or you may wish to expand one image into enormous detail.

What the A.I.M. Sequence Can Do for You

You will manage better, create more, and be happier by learning active relaxation, imagery, and mental rehearsal. Just as active relaxation is much different from merely sitting and reading in a reclining chair, imagery of the end result is more than merely daydreaming once in a while about a promotion or more money. And mental rehearsal is more effective than consciously practicing because you are also conditioning your unconscious mind to work on your behalf.

There are many practical benefits of using the A.I.M. strategy, such as more comfort and success at meetings or when speaking to large groups. Fear of public speaking is the most cited fear in the business and general population. Most CEOs and organization leaders must perform public speaking engagements from time to time. Here's an example of how one individual used the strategy to improve her public appearances.

Joan is marketing manager for a large fast-food restaurant chain. She always likes to work behind the scenes, and enjoys the strategic part of her job a great deal. One of her strengths was not public speaking. However, when an important industry event involving her company suddenly occurred, she became the person that the press wanted to speak to.

She was experienced at relaxation training from some past yoga exercising and an afternoon session of instruction in the Superskills. Joan quickly began active relaxation and imagery of each upcoming presentation or interview, including television. She found herself making positive changes from the second day. In a brief two weeks Joan was interviewed, held numerous press conferences, and made speeches to associations, all with practically no prior public speaking experience.

It is precisely this sort of quick reaction to surprises and positive outcomes that are the benefits that new workaholics enjoy. Along with that successful transformation, Joan felt elated and a savory taste of accomplishment. New workaholics, as we said earlier, most often work as much for the nonmonetary rewards of their careers, such as pride of accomplishment and the experience of success, as they do for promotions or money.

True optimal performers do not spin their wheels, waste time, nor are they in a hurry and getting nowhere. Hyperperformers may work long and intensely, but they accomplish their goals and are usually very time-efficient and productive. Just how productive can hyper-performers be? Here is a brief glimpse in the lives of some well known self-proclaimed new workaholics.

Ed Koch, Mayor of New York City, in one day dictated five newspaper columns, held two press conferences, chaired an estimates meeting, gave two luncheon speeches at two different hotels, convened three staff meetings, kicked off a Boy Scout fundraising campaign, helicoptered to the wake of a dead city fireman, and had dinner with friends. He commented that it wasn't a particularly busy day.

Robert Gallo, a top medical researcher at Bethesda Maryland Cancer Institute, works on AIDS research 72 hours a week. He holds meetings in elevators and during cross-town commutes to Capital Hill appointments.

It isn't surprising that Jesse Jackson worked 16 to 20 hours a day while campaigning for the Democratic presidential nomination, but what is noteworthy is that he has kept up that pace even after the election. He traveled 60,000 miles last year between his three bases of operation. He often gives five to seven speeches a day, and his press secretary says Jackson loves what he is doing, and doesn't consider himself hard-working.

In 1984 Cyndi Lauper worked 360 days and performed 300 concerts. That schedule covered 150 cities, including one stint of 10 cities in 10 days. While making her 3 videos that year, she put in 40 18-hour days. For a diversion, Cyndi manages a female wrestler.

Supreme Court Judge Sandra Day O'Connor frequently works six days a week. She entertains, plays tennis, and maintains an active family life.

Margaret Thatcher, when asked about being a workaholic said, "I was born that way and I was trained that way. I don't see how anyone can lie in the sun and do nothing all day."

Bill Marriott, head of the hotel chain that carries his name has stated that he comes from a long line of workaholics. He observes that there are a lot of millionaires today who didn't have any money 10 years ago, and Marriott thinks that's great. His corporate formula for success is "good people and hard work."

A survey published in the April 28, 1986 issue of *Fortune* showed that of the Fortune 500 CEOs the single largest group (46 percent) worked from 55 to 64 hours per week and 22 percent worked 65 or more hours per week. The study also showed that there is a major change in what are considered banker's hours. Seventy-one percent of CEOs from banking companies worked 55 hours per week or more.

Though working more than a 40-hour week is not a requirement to be a new workaholic, it does seem to be the case more often than not. The real indicator is that new workaholics produce and accomplish more in the hours they devote to their work than do SOPs.

Joe Charbonneau has been a regular speaker for over 10 years, and has been in the human development industry for 16 years. Prior to that, he was in the insurance business and had owned several beauty salons. He sold his company, Employer's Services Corporation, to the Traveler's Insurance Company, with a net of over one million dollars after taxes.

He puts in over 70 hours a week in Joe Charbonneau Presentations, Inc. and considers himself extremely happy. He has only been ill once in 20 years. But about 7 months after Joe sold Employer's Services Corporation, he was making a three-hour drive to a seminar when he became overwhelmed by a feeling of depression.

Now it might seem strange that someone who is fundamentally happy, a self-avowed workaholic who has just received a check for a million dollars, should be depressed. However, it is precisely because he is so happy doing his work that he became depressed over selling his business. There was a true sense of loss that Joe felt in selling his business. In fact, he even had seller's remorse a week before receiving the million dollar check. His depression was at the loss of what had made him happy for so many years.

His down period was short lived. As Joe geared up his new business in seminar presentations, he took swift and effective action to lift his mood.

To believe that new workaholics never become depressed or feel unhappy is unrealistically Polyanna-ish. It is the decisive and positive manner in which new workaholics deal with such ebbs in spirit that separate them from others.

The November 1985 issue of *Association Management* contained an article, "Better Management Through the Mind's Eye" by William P. Anthony, explaining how Anthony and his colleagues studied the use of imagery by executives. They believed that if athletes can benefit from imagery techniques, why not business executives? Their preliminary results reveal that managers can use imagery in a structured, conscious way to reach their business objectives.

"Events often do not turn out as we imagine, of course," Anthony points out, "because other people and unforeseen circumstances help shape the future. But mental imagery can increase the likelihood of success."

Dealing with Negative Experiences

When most of us work at making a change, practicing a new management skill, a new procedure, or a new professional technique, we often expect that it will go right for us the first time. However, it is quite natural that we may make some mistakes or otherwise not have it go well the first time. From such negative experiences some people begin to feel that subsequent attempts will also fail and thereby initiate the self-fulfilling prophecy.

Negative experiences or failures even in our daily work or on projects can leave behind a trace of negative expectancy and self-doubt. When we have such trace memories of unsuccessful events or attempts, we may be inhibited or unconsciously unsure of ourselves the next time out. For example, if you are in sales and have had several unsuccessful interviews or presentations, you may have a bit of self-doubt on subsequent calls. These can be mental land mines just waiting for your next footstep.

Individuals deal differently with unsuccessful events and circumstances. Some people can shrug off a minor failure or difficulty, and others are unable to let go of it for weeks or months. Fortunately, you can use imagery to mind sweep these and prevent them from interfering with future actions.

An effective way to interrupt that cycle is to selectively forget the unsuccessful experience. Learn everything you need from the experience, then forget about it. That's an abstract that needs to be put into practical application. An example of selective amnesia for negative results is that of Greg, a telecommunications consultant.

Professionally, Greg is very competent. However, he is in a rapidly transforming industry, and mistakes are made. Greg has developed a method by which he deals with such negative experiences. After first relaxing, he mentally pictures his mistake or the misguided event for a few minutes. He learns from it what he can, registers how to avoid it in the future, then he forgets it ever happened.

To clear his mind of the negativity of the event, Greg imagines it being placed into a trash bag, just as any item that is no longer useful. Very methodically, he mentally bundles the unpleasant experience and the rest of the trash and drops it into the trash chute. In his imagery he hears the bag fall and land in the receptacle far away from him. When he closes the door of the chute, he has closed the mental door on that negative event and the memory of it is as far away as the bag, and it gets further away as time passes.

Just as a real bag of garbage is hauled away, the mental garbage is removed from his mind. When Greg lets go of a memory in this manner, it is nearly erased from his conscious mind, and it is completely filed well away in his unconscious, as well.

There are times when one of his staff will ask him about a particular project that had trouble spots, and he gets a blank look because he has truly forgotten the incident. While such a nearly complete memory blot often takes considerable practice to accomplish, there will be some noticeable benefits from even beginning efforts.

Just as Greg took a scene from his real environment (the garbage bag and the trash chute) and used it for his mental rehearsal, your most effective imagery and mental pictures should incorporate scenes that are vivid and real to you. It is not important at all that such images may be totally implausible and impossible to accomplish in reality; your unconscious recognizes your intent and acts upon that intent regardless of how preposterous the mental scene might be.

Learning to Improve Your Imagery Skills

Skills are most easily learned from instructors who already know them, and who can teach either from a program or from their own experiences. This is true of most skills, whether learning pitching or batting from a coach, learning to play a musical instrument, understanding a new production technique from an equipment representative, a new manufacturing procedure, or a new sales or management skill from an experienced leader.

If you were a surgeon wishing to learn a new coronary bypass technique, to whom would you go for instruction? There may be no better place than the individuals who developed the procedure. The closer to the source of the knowledge, often the better the instruction.

It is possible to learn new skills on your own, though it may take more time. Trial and error are effective if somewhat inefficient. So how do you learn the imagery skills we are discussing? Certainly from a book such as this one, from a mentor, perhaps a professional in stress management and imagery, or from someone in your firm who has received direct training from skilled professionals.

However, regardless of how one acquires these techniques, you become better and more effective with practice and continued use. There are exercises that enhance your fundamental ability to use imagery.

First, imagine several cars, and examine the characteristics of each one. Then imagine the car you would like to have.

An exercise for improving your self-image is to imagine three picture frames. In the first picture frame imagine how you believe you are. In the second frame imagine how others see you and notice the differences between the first and second images. Of course, this is the place for complete honesty with yourself; no one will see these images but you. Then in the third picture frame imagine how you would like to appear. This is the goal or objective frame.

With those as beginning or starter exercises, here are eight categories of management activities for which mental imagery can be effectively applied.

1. Goal setting
2. Strategic strategizing—marketing, sales, production
3. Innovation and creative problem solving
4. Communication
5. Stress management
6. Career strategizing
7. Time organization
8. Interpersonal relations—superiors, subordinates, family

These are good areas in which to begin practicing imagery and mental rehearsal because many of them are also traits of optimal performers. Exercises for each of these categories can be created that use imagery to expand the unconscious involvement.

An exercise in strategic planning, for example, involves imagining yourself attending an industry conference five years in the future and imagining what the agenda issues would include. Then mentally picture the group discussing those issues while your mental facilitator compiles a list of the points uncovered during the exercise.

We have found that the combination of active relaxation, imagery of the completed goal, and mental rehearsal—the Superskills—is the sequence that allows the mental exercise just described to be most effective. The imagery exercises can be adapted to any situation and industry. Here is an example of how one individual uses imagery for planning purposes.

Jerry is the owner of a large commercial printing firm. During his strategic planning period each year he uses imagery to create a scenario of his trade association's annual conference held in Los Angeles. Jerry imagines what the agenda five years in the future will look like. He imagines what the topics will be and what the emphasis will be on. From that imagined list of topics and issues he imagines the suppliers, his competitors, all of the various groups that are represented at the conference and trade show. He imagines what new technology, what new equipment, and what market changes are evidenced by the program circular that he imagines holding in his hand.

From this future imagining, Jerry "blue skys" how the market might be five or six years ahead. For example, he may imagine a new piece of equipment. In his imagery he may have pulled from memory a story about new technology in waterless printing plates that last longer and have greater print characteristics than present plates.

"With the imagery, planning became easier for me because an undirected, abstract future was transformed into concrete ideas," Jerry commented. "Even though I came up with some really wild and impractical ideas, those may help spark some ideas that have merit and are useable."

In his imagined round-table discussions Jerry may find new possibilities for the future, but most importantly, he can put into his actual strategic plan allowances for upgrading his equipment and production capabilities to take advantage of his imagined changes in technology. This might seem somewhat risky to executives not accustomed to imagining the future. However, Jerry's imagining draws on input that is based upon reality. He is opening himself up to future possibilities that are likely to occur in some form or another. This is not to say that he will rush out to invest money in the first breed of new printing plates. Rather, he is preparing to take advantage of such technological innovations when they are likely to develop.

Because the human mind, when in a relaxed and imaginative state, is able to recall and process more options and possibilities, imagery strategic planning can be more productive. The difference is that when you use your conscious mind to plan, it may selectively edit ideas, future possibilities, and options that it deems unsubstantiated. As we know from history it is often the impossible idea that ultimately flies beyond the belief of overly rational people. Your imagination can calculate intuitive and irrational bits of information that can lead to breakthrough ideas and actions.

While hyper-performers may not surrender their good judgment to intuition and imagined possibilities, they will keep the doors open to unexpected events and capitalize on them when they do occur. Additionally, executives can imagine themselves five years in the future and imagine the age, sex, behavior, and attire of the customers in that future setting.

Such an exercise is a supplemental method in planning to keep ahead of the marketplace in new product development, financial planning, acquisitions, and innumerable aspects of development. For instance, Phillip is the CEO of a midwestern department store chain. Since retailing is very sensitive to the changing whims and preferences of the public, Phillip uses imagery to help him anticipate the changes in his customers and their tastes over a 3- to 5-year period. This is necessary to keep in style with his window displays, customer flow through a store, and other merchandising features.

He imagines what a customer will be like in five years. Phillip will take several imagery sessions to project a mental image of future customers. His composite will give him a clue as to the average age, color preferences, and buying attitudes of future shoppers. He may imagine whether future shoppers will be predominantly female or male.

As with Jerry in the printing industry, Phillip is not trying to second-guess the future. He is allowing his unconscious mind to assist him in putting together all the information and intelligence that presently exists to better read the future.

Quite a lot of what we as individuals are exposed to remains unused in our unconscious minds. Often when decision-making time arrives we may not remember all the tiny bits of intelligence we may have garnered. If we do not open up this vast library of material to be blended into the equation, we limit ourselves unnecessarily.

With imagery, we can access one of the most powerful resources we have at our disposal: our unconscious mind, our organic supercomputer. As we discussed earlier, more options allow your unconscious to make selections and decisions based upon your goals.

Anthony's study involved an exercise in which the executives were asked to imagine shooting arrows into a target some 50 yards away. In their imagery they were to sharply detail business targets 3 years ahead.

An exercise for creative problem-solving had the executives imagining themselves eating an artichoke, each leaf representing a symptom of the problem. As they ate more of the leaves they moved closer to the heart of the problem, and by eating the heart of the artichoke they digested and resolved the problem. This exercise encouraged them to recognize and concentrate on the core problem rather than becoming distracted by the symptoms.

To improve time organization imagine yourself going through a typical workday in slow motion and in minute detail. You could then better analyze where you were wasting time, where you were most effective, where you can delegate tasks and responsibilities, and how you can handle interruptions and set better schedules for yourself.

This form of imagined examination of your work habits and routines is useful in several ways. First, by imagining yourself in the work setting you allow your unconscious mind to select what items will be imagined. You may be surprised to find that you are focusing on events, tasks, or people you might have thought were insignificant or that you had forgotten about. The fact that your unconscious mind has included them in your imagined day might indicate that those events, small projects, or personal interactions have more meaning than you might otherwise have thought. With that insight you could probe a bit deeper to find what importance they might have. Keep a note pad or tape recorder handy while you relax and practice an imagery experience to record impressions or ideas.

Second, by slowing down and closely reviewing your actions, reactions, and routines you may find areas of your workday that can be streamlined or modified to be more effective. For example, your imagined procedure for conducting a meeting with your staff might show you that you could be better prepared for dealing with interpersonal conflicts between staff members. You might find that people are sending you signals that you have missed.

Again, your imagery of these past meetings and even of contact you had with the participants outside of the meetings registered in your unconscious perceptions. It can be those unconscious impressions that are most valuable to a successful executive because more complete information often produces better decisions and plans.

Does Age Affect Use of the Superskills?

Business Week, on March 31, 1986, reported that Robert Anderson, Rockwell International's chairman of the board, is past 60 years old, and says he has little left to prove. Since he became CEO in 1974 the company has tripled in size. Sales reached $11.3 billion in 1985 and earnings jumped five-fold to $600 million. However, Anderson has no intention of abandoning his 18-hour workday.

As reported in *Inc.* magazine, in June 1986, Geno Paulucci, the frozen pizza magnate who sold his business to Pillsbury for $200 million, and a land developer at 67 years old, is also launching a new quick-pizza business. He sells his businesses before he has to manage them.

George Burns said, "I'm going to stay in show business until I'm the only one left." He has made 25 films, thousands of personal appearances, and written five books. George prides himself on never taking a vacation because he loves what he does so much that not working would seem like a punishment. George Burns is over 90 years old.

Last year, at 81 years of age, Bob Hope scheduled more than 250 appearances, and though that seems like a heavy load, he said, "I'm only doing the things I like to do."

Barbara Cartland wrote 23 books last year. So far she has written 403 romance novels, 3 cookbooks, 5 biographies, and 1 children's book. She produces nearly a chapter a day, writes 600 letters a month, and operates a mail-order business. Barbara celebrated her 83rd birthday last year.

William Henry Gates, 30, Chairman of Microsoft Corporation, developed the computer operating system used by all IBM personal computers. *Money* magazine, in its July 1986 issue, reported that Gates no longer works 24 hours in a row as he previously did, but still maintains a 65-hour work week.

What these individuals have in common is joy in their work, which some refuse to even call work. They are truly happy at their *chosen* professions, and for the most part would rather work than take a vacation or work at something else. That feeling of contentment in their vocation and the perception that their vocation is really an avocation is fundamental to being a new workaholic. When individuals receive so much pleasure from their work that they look forward to getting to it, they are almost always more effective than workers who put in lots of time because they have little else to do.

Being in control is one element that allows new workaholics to develop such intensity and pleasure in their endeavors. After all, as we have said all along, new workaholics are happy; to be happy one must first *want* to be happy.

Before moving on to additional tactics for improving the 10 traits of hyper-performance, we will provide an assessment opportunity of those characteristics with the Personal Inventory Profile™.

The Personal Inventory Profile™

This questionnaire is designed to evaluate your present status in the 10 traits of hyper-performance.

Answer the questions below by circling your response: R = Rarely, S = Sometimes, O = Often, or A = Almost Always.

A1   I can't wait to wake up in the morning and get ready to start the day.

R   S   O   A

A2   In conversations my words are deliberate and thought-out before I express them.

                                    R   S   O   A

A3   Many situations and people excite me.

                                    R   S   O   A

A4   My life is dull.

                                    R   S   O   A

A5   In usual conversations I talk rapidly and with much emotion.

                                    R   S   O   A

A6   It is important to me to be relaxed and passive in most situations.

                                    R   S   O   A

B1   I really like my work and would do it even if I didn't have to work to support myself.

                                    R   S   O   A

B2   When I retire I will do all the things I want to do.

                                    R   S   O   A

B3   I know these are the best of times.

                                    R   S   O   A

B4   I believe that if I had a better education, parents, or more money I would be more successful.

                                    R   S   O   A

B5   I would rather be where I am now than where I was any time in my past.

                                    R   S   O   A

B6 At night I wake up and have trouble getting back to sleep.

$$\text{R} \quad \text{S} \quad \text{O} \quad \text{A}$$

C1 I get what I want if I help others get what they want.

$$\text{R} \quad \text{S} \quad \text{O} \quad \text{A}$$

C2 I like my profession mostly because it brings me respect, control, and/or monetary rewards.

$$\text{R} \quad \text{S} \quad \text{O} \quad \text{A}$$

C3 Trying my best at work makes a difference.

$$\text{R} \quad \text{S} \quad \text{O} \quad \text{A}$$

C4 I feel that I'm not where I want to be in my career or my personal life because I'm not lucky.

$$\text{R} \quad \text{S} \quad \text{O} \quad \text{A}$$

C5 I believe my worth comes not from what I do but from what I am.

$$\text{R} \quad \text{S} \quad \text{O} \quad \text{A}$$

C6 I believe people will do better if you tell them what they are doing wrong.

$$\text{R} \quad \text{S} \quad \text{O} \quad \text{A}$$

D1 I finish what I start.

$$\text{R} \quad \text{S} \quad \text{O} \quad \text{A}$$

D2 I am too easily distracted from tasks I begin.

$$\text{R} \quad \text{S} \quad \text{O} \quad \text{A}$$

D3 Things turn out all right when I keep working at them.

$$\text{R} \quad \text{S} \quad \text{O} \quad \text{A}$$

D4 I want to be successful, but I believe there are too many obstacles in my way.

$$\text{R} \quad \text{S} \quad \text{O} \quad \text{A}$$

D5 I believe it is the little things I do that lead to large results.

$$R \quad S \quad O \quad A$$

D6 I don't accomplish as much as I want to because there are too many interruptions.

$$R \quad S \quad O \quad A$$

E1 I regularly read magazines and books in fields not related to mine.

$$R \quad S \quad O \quad A$$

E2 I need to have a project finished before undertaking another one.

$$R \quad S \quad O \quad A$$

E3 I am considered a Renaissance person.

$$R \quad S \quad O \quad A$$

E4 I feel that there are two ways to do things, a right way and a wrong way.

$$R \quad S \quad O \quad A$$

E5 I believe even the most absurd conclusions may have merit.

$$R \quad S \quad O \quad A$$

E6 I believe humor is only appropriate in certain situations.

$$R \quad S \quad O \quad A$$

F1 I regularly practice a relaxation technique.

$$R \quad S \quad O \quad A$$

F2 I like setting up precise routines and following them.

$$R \quad S \quad O \quad A$$

F3   People are basically trustworthy.

R   S   O   A

F4   It is important that I don't make mistakes.

R   S   O   A

F5   I change jobs, even if within the same company, at least once every five years.

R   S   O   A

F6   I feel that most so-called changes for the better really make things worse.

R   S   O   A

G1   I feel comfortable using personal contacts or connections to get things accomplished.

R   S   O   A

G2   I believe I could accomplish more if only I knew influential people.

R   S   O   A

G3   There are people I can talk to about almost any business or personal problem.

R   S   O   A

G4   I find it difficult to meet new people.

R   S   O   A

G5   What I don't know, but need to know, I learn or find the answers to somehow.

R   S   O   A

G6   I feel that I am not knowledgeable enough about fields unrelated to my work.

R   S   O   A

H1   I look at the bright side of situations.

$$\text{R} \quad \text{S} \quad \text{O} \quad \text{A}$$

H2   I know I would be happy if I had more money.

$$\text{R} \quad \text{S} \quad \text{O} \quad \text{A}$$

H3   I take care of my body with healthier food and regular exercise.

$$\text{R} \quad \text{S} \quad \text{O} \quad \text{A}$$

H4   I miss five or more days from work each year due to illness or accidents.

$$\text{R} \quad \text{S} \quad \text{O} \quad \text{A}$$

H5   There is at least one benefit from any problem.

$$\text{R} \quad \text{S} \quad \text{O} \quad \text{A}$$

H6   I believe if something can go wrong it will (Murphy's Law).

$$\text{R} \quad \text{S} \quad \text{O} \quad \text{A}$$

I1   I write down my goals.

$$\text{R} \quad \text{S} \quad \text{O} \quad \text{A}$$

I2   I feel that goals are only for people who need them.

$$\text{R} \quad \text{S} \quad \text{O} \quad \text{A}$$

I3   I regularly take time to visualize my goals.

$$\text{R} \quad \text{S} \quad \text{O} \quad \text{A}$$

I4   I find myself thinking, "Is this all there is from life?"

$$\text{R} \quad \text{S} \quad \text{O} \quad \text{A}$$

I5   I know precisely what I want from life.

$$\text{R} \quad \text{S} \quad \text{O} \quad \text{A}$$

I6   I feel that life is usually, "Another day, another dollar."

R S O A

J1   I frequently do two or more things at the same time.

R S O A

J2   My life seems like everything's a crisis.

R S O A

J3   I have enough time to do what is important to me.

R S O A

J4   I can't do anything new because I can barely keep up with my daily work schedule.

R S O A

J5   I learn at least one new skill every year.

R S O A

J6   With me, procrastination is a way of life.

R S O A

Scoring: Transfer your answers to the charts that follow by taking your answers to odd-numbered questions, such as A1, B3, etc., and assigning $R=1$, $S=3$, $O=5$, $A=7$. Assign even-numbered questions, such as A2, B4, etc., $R=7$, $S=5$, $O=3$, $A=1$. Total your points in each column. Then convert your totals to the 1 to 10 rating scale. You will have a rating scale for each of the 10 new workaholic characteristics. These will give you an indication of your present new workaholic traits level.

PASSION

	R	S	O	A
A1				
A2				
A3				
A4				
A5				
A6				
Totals	___ +	___ +	___ +	___ = ___

PRESENT CENTERED

	R	S	O	A
B1				
B2				
B3				
B4				
B5				
B6				
Totals	___ +	___ +	___ +	___ = ___

PERSONAL POWER

	R	S	O	A
C1				
C2				
C3				
C4				
C5				
C6				
Totals	___ +	___ +	___ +	___ = ___

PERSEVERANCE

	R	S	O	A
D1				
D2				
D3				
D4				
D5				
D6				
Totals	__ +	__ +	__ +	__ = __

CREATIVITY

	R	S	O	A
E1				
E2				
E3				
E4				
E5				
E6				
Totals	__ +	__ +	__ +	__ = __

ADAPTABLE

	R	S	O	A
F1				
F2				
F3				
F4				
F5				
F6				
Totals	__ +	__ +	__ +	__ = __

RESOURCEFUL

	R	S	O	A
G1				
G2				
G3				
G4				
G5				
G6				
Totals	__ +	__ +	__ +	__ = __

OPTIMISTIC

	R	S	O	A
H1				
H2				
H3				
H4				
H5				
H6				
Totals	__ +	__ +	__ +	__ = __

GOAL SETTING

	R	S	O	A
I1				
I2				
I3				
I4				
I5				
I6				
Totals	__ +	__ +	__ +	__ = __

141

TIME EFFICIENCY

	R	S	O	A
J1				
J2				
J3				
J4				
J5				
J6				
Totals	__ +	__ +	__ +	__ = __

For each of the above characteristics convert the total points of all four columns for each trait to the rating from 0 to 10 from the conversion table below:

40–42 points places you at 10 on the rating scale
36–39 points places you at 9 on the rating scale
32–35 points places you at 8 on the rating scale
28–34 points places you at 7 on the rating scale
25–27 points places you at 6 on the rating scale
22–24 points places you at 5 on the rating scale
18–22 points places you at 4 on the rating scale
14–21 points places you at 3 on the rating scale
10–13 points places you at 2 on the rating scale
 7– 9 points places you at 1 on the rating scale
   6 points places you at 0 on the rating scale

RATING SCALE FOR EACH HYPER-PERFORMANCE TRAIT

SOP   HYPER-PERF

0   1   2   3   4 | 5 | 6   7   8   9   10

6

*Designing Your Personal
Mental Fitness™ Program*

*A*pplying the basic techniques of the A.I.M. program will produce results if you practice regularly without an individualized program. However, when you develop a program and an overall strategy, the A.I.M. plan becomes dynamic, and its effectiveness is enhanced by a large measure.

In order to design a program that addresses and develops specific optimal performance traits, you must begin with the assessment provided earlier to determine where you presently are regarding the 10 traits of optimal performers. Once you have established these benchmarks from the Personal Inventory Profile™ evaluation in Chapter 5, you can then use the A.I.M. Strategy to focus on those traits that will produce the most results in the shortest time. In a way, it is like creating a road map that you can use to find the shortest distance from where you are to where you want to be.

One key difference between a new workaholic and a stressed-out person is that new workaholics are generally happy about what they are doing and don't see their work as a monkey on their back. Being happy about your lifestyle and your career is essential to avoiding illness and to achieving high levels of performance.

Another valuable assessment tool is to record your perceptions of your own optimal performance qualities. This assessment is essential for you to determine which traits you wish to work on first and most intently. As you develop your overall A.I.M. program, use the Hyper-Performance Strategies in Chapter 3 to select the specific skills, strategies, knowledge building methods, and miscellaneous techniques for enhancing specific traits.

Without some form of accurate gauge of where your strengths and weaknesses are and what type of personality you presently reflect, you may misjudge what areas in your professional life you need to develop.

The Importance of Designing a
Plan for Yourself

No successful entrepreneur begins a new business without a business plan to follow. Though that plan is often modified as the business progresses, to begin without one would leave one to trial and error, missed opportunities, and general inefficiency, among other things. To begin implementing changes in your business and personal life, and to develop new success skills and eliminate negative characteristics without a thought-out program, is somewhat like starting a business without a plan. It can be done, but not as efficiently.

An example of trying to do the right thing without such a program is that of Donald, vice president of finance at a large computer software developer. For most of his life he considered himself to be a Type B personality. He seemed to enjoy his leisure time and often took vacations with his family. He believed he found satisfaction in his work without a weighty sense of competition. Donald was usually thoughtful and contemplative, yet could easily become competitive when the situation required it.

Yet, Donald was missing something in his life, or something was present that he couldn't explain. Instead of being a calm, relaxed person, which Type B somewhat suggests, he felt stressed, tense, and keyed-up much of the time, even right after a vacation. He believed that relaxation came from a vacation or time off with his family.

In reality, for Donald, a vacation was taking him away from

what he truly enjoyed—his work. He was very competent at his profession and an achiever. However, he felt that possessing the Type B traits were healthier. He was reacting to the earlier concepts that all Type A personalities were heart-attack prone.

When we began seeing Donald, we helped him develop a personal A.I.M. program. Active relaxation was something he was not accustomed to practicing. However, through active relaxation Donald found that his energy level increased, his speech pace quickened, he began thinking and doing several things at once and with positive results.

Donald demonstrated to himself that there was more to the Type A personality than what was popularly known. He was taking on more of the Type A characteristics as a result of his active relaxation, his end-result imagery of specific objectives, and his mental rehearsal of task processes.

What is worth noting is that not all characteristics of the Type A personality are negative and not all the Type B traits are positive. Donald was learning to select those Type A traits that produced better overall performance while avoiding the characteristics of hostility, anger, and lack of control that would jeopardize his health. That is precisely the value of the A.I.M. Strategy.

We encourage you to use the relaxation skills from Chapter 3 to gain an ability to drain off excessive stress and practice your imagery skills to first establish goals and priorities for yourself.

Earlier we described the 10 traits of hyper-performers and provided some examples of how the A.I.M. Superskills can be used to enhance and develop those traits. In this chapter we will discuss specific tactics for using imagery and mental rehearsal for creating specific changes in those 10 areas. The other actions and techniques described in the Hyper-performers Success Formula in Chapter 3 are valuable, but imagery and mental rehearsal can provide both immediate and long-term benefits for improving your performance.

The examples and tactics for imagery and mental rehearsal provided here are not meant to be all-inclusive. Rather they are intended as starting points for you to spring from in creating a full program for yourself. By starting with what is provided here you will develop the skill to imagine additional approaches that are taken from your own background and experiences.

In our workshops we ask participants questions about their likes, hobbies, favorite movies, favorite foods, and a host of other questions intended to provide personal material from which imagery can be developed that will be relevant to that individual. You can do that for yourself, also. The imagery that is most effective feels most in line with images that are familiar to your unconscious. You hold the keys to that familiarity.

Imagery or Mental Rehearsal?

As you develop tactics for specific trait enhancement or for a specific task, project, or event you have ahead of you, you will likely come upon a situation where either imagery or mental rehearsal seems inappropriate. For example, developing optimism is not easy to do using rehearsal techniques. Rather, end-result imagery is much more fitting. When this situation occurs simply use whichever seems the easiest to utilize. It is rare to find a situation where result imagery cannot be used. It is the more powerful of the two imaging techniques, so use it first and whenever you can.

Often what you will find works well is a combination of the two. As you mentally rehearse a series of events they will culminate in a result. That is a wonderful blend. Much like a basketball player would rehearse receiving a pass, then executing a fake motion and a hook shot, the imagery would always be resolved with the ball going in the basket.

You will also notice that we have provided examples of both generic trait enhancement and specific task situations. In your personal program you will want to work on both. If, for instance, you desire to improve your creativity, use imagery to develop better general creative habits; but also, you will have specific creative projects that you will want to work on. The same basic procedures can be adapted to both.

Material for Your Own Mental Fitness™ Program

Passion

As we pointed out earlier, passion can also be described as commitment, enthusiasm, and excitement toward your work or toward a project you may be involved in. Enthusiasm for your work can be a critical factor in whether you are perceived to be successful or not. Aside from changing careers or other radical moves to generate commitment and passion, there is an effective tactic for bringing enthusiasm to your work and utilizing your past successes. Imagine a past situation in which you were excited, enthused.

An example could be a sporting event in which you became so involved and excited you screamed and yelled for your favorite team or player. Recall that situation in your imagination and mentally relive that experience, noting the feeling you had and the positive aspects of it, including the physical and mental aspects.

Perhaps you became excited when you first began your present position. Recall how good that feeling was and explore in your imagination what it was about the new job that excited you. Was it the challenge, the opportunities, the feeling of accomplishment? In recapturing those feelings and exploring the elements you can gain insight into how you can recreate those feelings here and now—in the present moment.

This is a situation where end-result imagery can work very well. When you have recalled the feelings of enthusiasm you once had, imagine that you now have that same excitement in your present work and what the results of that excitement would be. Perhaps imagine comments from colleagues, superiors, or subordinates; imagine those comments, imagine yourself feeling excited about going to work in the morning, or even contrast your enthusiasm with that of someone you recognize who lacks passion, someone who gets religion twice a week as in "Thank God it's Friday," and "Oh my God, it's Monday."

Mentally picture yourself excited about your current work, anxious to get back to it, committed to seeing it completed. As Aaron Beck described in the form of cognitive therapy, thoughts (even those in your imagery) create feelings, and feelings create actions. Repeated imagery of this type will produce emotional and physical changes. You will have more energy, and that energy will translate into more excitement toward your work. The excitement and enthusiasm will create actions that will be recognized as commitment and passion.

Adaptability

You will find that recalling past successes, as with the above example of developing passion and enthusiasm, is effective in many other situations. Developing more adaptability is similar. When was the last time you were dramatically adaptable? When you received a promotion? When you got married? When you moved into a new home in a new neighborhood? These might provide examples of how you handled the need to be flexible and adaptable.

With the mental picture of how adaptable you have been in a past situation, use that in your present situation. Suppose that you needed to adapt to a new client's personality. Mentally rehearse how you can be confident, congenial, relaxed, exhibiting all the social skills you possess. Imagine talking with that client and asking questions that elicit positive responses and how good you feel at being flexible enough to cultivate a new relationship with someone for whom you may not really care in the beginning.

You might also relate your present situation to other forms of adaptation you are familiar with. For example, the penguin adapted to being a flightless, aquatic bird that is now capable of many things other birds are not, such as swimming underwater for long periods of time in freezing water. You may find that if long-term adaptation to new conditions is required, relating to an image such as that provides a type of abstract role model to follow.

As silly as it may seem, you might see yourself as an Imperial Penguin, a large creature able to withstand conditions that would kill many other species. Yet you, like that penguin, are able to adapt to new market conditions, a new product line, new people. Such imagery can further relate to the evolutionary characteristics. First, make some small adjustments, maybe one action per day that leads toward a specific objective.

Decide what your final goal and intermediate goals are and image progressive steps of change if that is appropriate. Suppose you wish to be more adaptable to new co-workers, but you have difficulty in relating to new people. You might begin by mentally rehearsing how you can take just one positive action each day to improve your relationship with a new colleague or superior. Rehearse one positive encounter, the question you might ask, the possible answers you might receive, the conversation that would follow, and the final result you seek. Perhaps the final daily result might be mutual smiles and a pleasant, comfortable departure.

Remember, small, incremental results that lead to bigger ones are the way to effect major changes. Relating your present desires to positive past experiences or to familiar examples is a key to effecting present changes.

Present-Centered

Being present-centered is a valuable asset that can produce noticeable results in a very short time of imagery practice. It is surprising that many people are not aware of how often they drift in and out of the present moment and how that affects their performance.

In a recent football game the San Diego Chargers were playing the Denver Broncos. John Elway threw a pass from the San Diego 11-yard line to one of his wide receivers just over the goal line. The receiver bobbled an easy catch and then dropped it with no defender even close. The television commentator, a former player, jokingly said the receiver had too much to do: think about how he was going to spike the ball, smile at the five photographers in the corner of the field, all sorts of things, and also catch the ball.

What the commentator was saying was that the receiver was *not* in the present moment; he was thinking about the few seconds in the future and his moment of glory. Sports offer many examples of the need to focus concentration on the present moment, not the few minutes or seconds just past or those yet to come. However, the same principles hold true in many business situations.

Certainly you experience present centering many times, at important meetings, during telephone conversations, or while working on an absorbing project or task. It will be surprisingly easy for you to recall such examples while in a relaxed imagery session. Recreate in your imagination how focused and attentive you were, how you were able to pick up nuances of someone's words and tones of voice, or gestures.

Often it is the subtle nonverbal communications that can make the difference between understanding and really understanding, or between a negotiation turning out well or terrifically.

After you have recalled several occasions when you were centered in the present and focused on what you were immediately involved in, find some cue or signal that will remind you to check your thoughts for present centering. For example, use the ringing of the telephone as a cue. Imagine yourself in a familiar setting. The telephone rings; that ringing signals you to focus your attention on the conversation exclusively.

To be more present-centered in a meeting you may wish to use the act of your sitting down as a cue to settle yourself and pay attention to what you are doing and to where you are. By mentally rehearsing such events in your imagery practice you are setting up unconscious as well as conscious cues for centering. The cues you develop can be anything in your environment or something you carry inside you: a word, a deep breath, the opening of your briefcase, any mental or physical action that will focus your attention on the present.

As you repeat the imagery of such signals and their successful results, in subsequent practice the cues become stronger until the response will occur more, if not totally, unconsciously than at a conscious level. To effect a positive change in this trait your awareness at a conscious level is initially essential, but the value of present centering becomes even greater as you develop an unconscious awareness of the present. The cues serve to help transfer that control from conscious to unconscious.

Resourcefulness

Your resourcefulness becomes most important, or at least most visible, when there is a specific problem to be solved.

How many times have you heard the comment that someone was very resourceful in remedying a situation. As a culture, we place a value on resourcefulness. In the business environment it can be a tremendous asset.

As we stated earlier, being resourceful is the trait of bringing together people, material, ideas, money, skills, information, and other components to make things happen and to achieve goals. Often the beginnings of such actions occur in brainstorming meetings. Of course, what would be ideal is to have such a meeting with individuals of very high caliber. Unfortunately such individuals are not accessible to everyone, or are they?

One effective tactic to improve your resourcefulness is to imagine a brainstorming session. However, in this mental setting you can invite anyone you wish. You can select anyone real or fictional who might be able to help you with the task or problem at hand.

First, equip yourself with a pad and pen or tape recorder so that all ideas or possibilities can be saved. In your imagery have each of your imagined participants comment on how they viewed the objective and what they thought could be useful in achieving it. You might imagine Henry Kissinger or Jesse Jackson; you could have leaders from your industry, members of your own organization, fictional heroes, or friends attending your brain trust. The key is to imagine what *they* would suggest or comment.

The technique is to open yourself up to allow all the possibilities into your unconscious. In this way you may find that the resources you need are within your grasp, or you may learn where you can go to obtain what you need.

Another tactic that is particularly effective when you seem to have run into a stone wall or the end of the road, figuratively, of course, is to mentally break down the barriers and open up a new road. Imagine yourself behind a wall or fenced area, except that you have the ability to dismantle the wall or melt the fence. Imagine the barrier in as much detail as you can, feel the material it is made of, see it if you can, hear it if that is possible. Include all five senses to the best of your ability in your imagery.

If you need tools to tear the wall down, imagine what those would be. A piece of equipment, a helper, or other assistance you imagine may represent the resource you are looking for or one that you have had all along, but didn't recognize.

While you are in a quiet, relaxed state, mentally picturing a scene like the one described above, you should take note of all that is said, all that is suggested, even if it may appear at first to be too ridiculous to work. Often such far reaches will prove to be the seeds of an idea or avenue that will produce results. You will want to review these notes or recordings later to see where the threads lead.

WILL TAKING PHYSICAL ACTION DURING IMAGERY DISRUPT THE SESSION?

When we recommend writing notes or speaking into a recorder while practicing imagery, the question often arises about what to do if the imagery experience is disrupted by the action of writing or speaking. We take notes and speak into a small recorder quite often during imagery for this application of resourcefulness. You may at first find that the mental picture is momentarily lost when you divert your attention to paper or recorder. Merely return to the imagery as soon as the note has been made.

After you have practiced the Superskills for a short time you will find that images will come and go and return very easily. The few moments it takes to record an idea or thought seldom disrupts the session for long. Speaking will soon become a comfortable activity that fits in with your eyes closed imagery. Naturally, this could seem odd if you are in an airport terminal or other public place, so we recommend jotting down a note on a piece of paper in those situations.

Personal Power

Developing your personal power is a matter of recognizing the personal power you already have and allowing yourself to exercise it. Power is often related more to perceptions than to anything tangible. Remember we are talking about your personal power to accomplish things, to influence people, and to get what you want, rather than the sort of power an elected official, a judge, or a law enforcement officer has.

Your personal power comes from within you. It is your ability to persuade, to create excitement, to get the things that you want. In practical business terms it often means not being intimidated by someone in a negotiation, accomplishing something outside the conventional system, or gathering others to your side of a policy or proposal.

A great deal of personal power emanates from the amount of self-confidence you possess. As you are more self-confident, others feel confident in your opinions and decisions and are more willing to be on your side. Your self-confidence also allows you to maintain your position in a negotiation without over-compromising to arrive at an agreement.

There are several tactics you can use to engender the self-confidence and perception of power that you may need. If you are in an arena of negotiation (this could be any sales situation or business forum), you can create more power for yourself if you perceive less power in the other participants. One way to do this is to imagine your counterparts as being the opposite of what they may seem.

For example, if you are going to meet with someone who is known to be gruff, powerful, and a tough negotiator, you can mentally picture that person in a clown costume. Or, if your opponent is an inflexible individual who makes no compromises, you can imagine him to be rubbery, malleable, and perhaps even fluid. By using imagery in which your target person is the opposite of what he or she is known to be, you set up a series of positive expectations for yourself.

If you perceive yourself as timid, weak, or ineffective, mentally picture yourself as perhaps a large bear, a powerful lion, or as a person whom you think of as a powerful role model: General Patton, the CEO of a major corporation, or anyone who you see as able to accomplish what you seek.

By establishing this positive expectancy and ascribing to your unconscious self the power to accomplish what you desire, you will be setting into motion elements of behavioral change that produce new actions.

HOW YOUR THOUGHTS AFFECT YOUR FEELINGS AND YOUR ACTIONS

Aaron Beck, in *Cognitive Therapy of Depression,* championed the case that thoughts create feelings, and that by changing the process of cognitive thoughts, we change the feelings that result from them. Earlier it was believed that feelings create thoughts, that if you felt depressed you would develop and hold onto negative, depressing thoughts. Beck believed the reverse. Put simply, Beck believed that if you both consciously and unconsciously process positive, constructive thoughts, then you will feel happier, more productive, more enthusiastic, more creative, more powerful, and so on. Sales training and motivational speakers have been using just that strategy for years, with generally positive results. Thoughts create feelings and feelings lead to actions.

Use imagery to create new ways of thinking about a person or a situation and your feelings will change. As your feelings change your actions will follow. So, if you are meeting with someone you initially believe to have more personal power than yourself, begin by imagining the reverse. As your imagery creates a new perception, you will feel differently and you will then act in a manner consistent with your feelings.

This tactic changes your perception of yourself. As you feel more confident you will act more so.

Another form of imagery to provide you with a greater sense of personal power is to imagine yourself sitting in a place where you feel comfortable, safe, and alone. Mentally picture the sun shining on you, causing you to feel warm, and imagine the sun's rays coming into you and bringing energy, just as it does for plants. Imagine that you can breathe in the sun's energy and that as you take deep, comfortable breaths, you are also taking in energy, confidence, and mental strength.

In some cases you may notice an increase in comfort and confidence very quickly, and in others it may take some time before results are observed or felt. Do not become discouraged if results take time to develop. Continue your imagery practice and try different variations on the tactics described above. They will work, but you must have tenacity and perseverance. If you need perseverance, that is the next trait we will discuss.

Perseverance

Perseverance can be applied to nearly every endeavor you are involved in; a love relationship, athletics, education, and of course, business and entrepreneurial pursuits. To persevere you need to have two things: a goal that you are trying to achieve, and the mind-set to disregard setbacks, failures, and difficulty. Have you ever heard the saying, "If it were easy, everyone would do it"? It is the tenacity to hang in there when others become discouraged, tired, or just lose interest that allows some to succeed while others give up and do something easier.

High-level achievers reach outstanding heights because they can find some way to continue even when there appears to be no progress. It is that seeming blindness to the possibility of total failure that separates winners from the "just-abouts," those who just about make it but stop short because of a setback or stall.

How can imagery help you persist? There are several ways, but take the case of Lin Shih-kum, the pianist who won second place in the prestigious International Tchaikovsky Competition in 1958. He came in second to Van Cliburn that year. What eventually happened to the slender, six-foot Chinese pianist is difficult to believe but true.

After winning the second prize in the competition, he returned to China. In 1965 Shih-kum was a well known concert pianist when Mao Tse-Tung and the Cultural Revolution came along. The Revolution was a bloody purge against anything and everything of Western influence, including music. Lin Shih-kum, for refusing to denounce the concert music he loved, was labeled an enemy of the people and was jailed. The beating he received when jailed cracked a bone in his forearm. He was locked away where he could not be seen.

For the next six years Shih-kum was confined in a small prison cell with no books to read, no paper to write on, and, of course, no piano. Then one day, for propaganda reasons, he was released and requested to perform in Peking with the Philadelphia Orchestra. The request came from the same Mao Tse-Tung who had had him jailed and beaten six years earlier.

His performance with the Philadelphia Orchestra was brilliant. How had he been able to play so well after six years without a piano, or even paper to write music on? He had played on a piano produced in his imagination and played as faithfully and as long as he would have had he had a piano.

That is a very specific application, and yet it could be used in other situations to improve or maintain skills you might be prevented from practicing otherwise. Are you studying for an advanced degree in your spare time? Are you prevented from assuming the responsibilities of a higher post for which you feel qualified? You can use imagery to maintain and enhance your skills and learning even when time or opportunity work against you.

It is said that Gordie Howe, the famous ice hockey player who played professionally until he was more than 50 years old, was an "ace bandage from his feet to his neck." He always played hurt. Some said that if he died he would miss only about three games. Perseverance was Howe's middle name.

FROM PAST TO PRESENT SUCCESS

A technique for helping you maintain your drive and forward movement during difficult times is to recall when you persevered and were successful. Can you remember training for a sports achievement, or how you persevered through college, or how you put up with visiting relatives for an unbearably long time? No matter how little your perseverance paid off, and regardless of how long you had to endure, recall the feelings of success you felt. Examine your prior experience and absorb into your imagined recall all the sensations you had: the elation of having done it, the praise you may have received, the sounds of the spectators, the taste of the victory champagne.

Relate those previous successes to the one you will have now as you continue in your work, your project, or whatever you are presently involved in. Imagine the feelings, sights,

...h wider field of creative selection than in your conscious
...king.

...any of the world's greatest discoveries were incubated
...ng imagery in the discoverer's imagination. In James
...son's book, *The Double Helix,* he tells of breaking the
...tic code using a mental rotation of the genetic elements.
...mes Maxwell reported making a mental picture of every
...lem. He arrived at his theory of classical electromag-
...m and the accompanying equations only after conjuring
...series of mentally pictured models.
...velist Joan Didion reported that her plots developed
...what she called "pictures in my mind." Judith Guest,
...wrote *Ordinary People,* says her novel began as a mental
...

...imagery tactic you can use to open yourself up to more
...ve possibilities is to imagine a large pond or lake. Float-
...the pond are inner tubes, lilies, or whatever platforms
...e. Imagine yourself getting closer to the floating plat-
...and one by one imagine something on them. Feel free
...ge what you mentally picture, alter it, let it fly up and
...r sink out of sight.
...ou develop this mental picture you can have the pond
...nt a problem, a goal, a product, a business, a group of
...or anything relevant to your business or personal life.
...ating objects can represent elements or possibilities.
...an excellent exercise during which to take notes. Al-
...r imagination to be totally free of physical restric-
...he reason for symbolizing the issue by something
...ferent, such as a pond, is that your imagination has
...edom to allow ideas and thoughts into the arena.
...r than a pond, imagine a blue sky with colored bal-
...a blank computer screen with many windows. The
...n be anything that you feel comfortable with. A
...ours who is an engineer used the image of a drawing

sounds, and tastes of success. Mentally picture yourself having already traversed the long road. Picture the end of the
long corridor and what the fruits of your patience and en-
durance will taste like.

As you imagine the rewards at the end of this particular
project or challenge, allow yourself to take on that feeling of
energy and elation. With regular practice you can maintain
your forward motion for as long as it takes to achieve your
desired results. Imagine each of your attempts, each day of
work without success or progress as steps closer to achievement. Thomas Edison, who had 150 failures at making a light
bulb before making one that worked, said, "I didn't fail 150
times, I learned 150 ways that will not work."

Optimism

A definition we like of an optimist is a fellow who takes cold
water thrown on his ideas, heats it with enthusiasm, makes
steam, and pushes ahead. Optimism and perseverance go
hand-in-hand. In Chapter 2 we provided some techniques for
generating an optimistic, positive attitude, and here we will
give you some additional methods utilizing imagery.

While in a relaxed state of mind, close your eyes and picture as many symbols of positive outcomes as you can. Here
are a few general symbols: the sun coming up after a stormy
night, getting well after a bad cold or case of the flu, your
favorite sports team winning the world championship, the last
time you received money you didn't expect, or being praised
for an accomplishment.

Open up your imagination and allow yourself to see and
perhaps even count all the ways a positive outcome is possible
on whatever work you are doing. Imagine negative outcomes
as crackers on the floor, or the peels from your favorite fruit.
You can sweep away or toss out those negative symbols.

Your imagery is a powerful way to begin a new way of feeling. If you push out negative thoughts from your unconscious and plant positive, optimistic ones you will actually feel more optimistic. The goal of your imagery for this characteristic is to feed positive, optimistic thoughts through your imagery and into your unconscious.

Optimism is helped by keeping a good sense of humor. We are reminded of the story of the father with two sons, one an optimist and one a pessimist. In order to see to what degree each possessed their particular trait, the father put them to a test. He locked the pessimistic son in a room with all the boy's favorite toys, and he put the optimistic son in a room with nothing but horse manure piled high. At the end of the day the father checked each room.

When he opened the first room and asked the pessimistic boy how his day had been the son replied, "Not very good. There are too many toys in here. I don't know what to play with first, and besides I'm afraid that if I played with the toys they might break."

When the father opened the second room he saw his optimistic son smiling, knee-deep and shoveling through a huge pile of horse manure. When he asked the boy what he was doing the son replied, "Dad, with all this horse manure I know you've hidden a pony in here somewhere."

Creativity

In Joseph Chilton Pearce's book, *The Crack in the Cosmic Egg*, he refers to creative insight as "Eureka!" He believes that such creativity comes about, in part, from opening ourselves up to possibilities not bound by even the physical reality in which we live. He offers that in our imaginations all solutions are possible. We need only create the physical parameters to allow the impossible to be possible.

How Can Imagery Help You Be Mor

In Chapter 2 we offered two steps to
first, opening yourself to as many possi
second, allowing time for incubation
gether in your unconscious of novel w
more known possibilities to form a n
five specific tactics for enhancing yo

1. Use your imagination to view pr
   perspective.

2. During your imagery write do
   ideas about a problem or situatio
   make no sense or that are irrel

3. Make intuitive conclusions and
   of the problem or objective.

4. Imagine several possible out
   poor. Then examine those out
   they could be changed. Write

5. Finally, leave the entire subje
   and do something totally u
   about the subject during tha
   laxed state of imagery and

Harold J. Leavitt, in *Corpor*
ativity is sometimes generated
the mind and forgetting a de
ambiguity and leave an issue
conscious to pull together ele
overlooked or discarded bec

A crucial feature of using
main nonjudgmental. As w
scious mind is free of the
As you stay in contact with

board and imagined himself seated and busy sketching. He could come into that image with shapes already drawn on the paper or picture himself drawing new shapes and designs.

The more ideas and potentials you can dream up, the more likely you are to arrive at unique combinations. And if you keep your judgment of possibilities out of the picture then you are encouraging more ideas and the circle gets larger, until "Eureka!"

Goal Setting

We mentioned in Chapter 2 that a written set of specific goals was essential for you to enlist your unconscious to work toward those objectives, and that these written goals form a personal contract with yourself.

A further gauge of how you are doing regarding setting specific, positive, achievable goals is to answer the following questions:

1. Do I have written, specific goals in my professional life for the next month, year, two years, five years, ten years?
2. Do I talk positively about my objectives to others, speaking in a manner that implies that I will attain my objectives?
3. Do I imagine myself once a day or more, having already attained my objectives?
4. Are my objectives high but still reachable? Are they beyond my grasp, but not beyond my reach?

If you have not honestly answered yes to all these questions then you may not be utilizing your goal-setting abilities to their highest potential. Take time to think about and write down your goals and objectives clearly and specifically.

John Naisbett says that strategic planning is worthless unless there is a strategic vision—a clear image of what it is you want to achieve.

There are two aspects to using imagery for your goals. One is developing goals and the other is achieving them.

CHARTING YOUR COURSE

First, if you are having difficulty developing specific goals for yourself, use imagery in the following exercise. Select a time and place to relax and be undisturbed for 30 or 40 minutes and use the active relaxation exercise in Chapter 4 to unwind and become as stress-free and comfortable as you can. Have a pen and paper or a tape recorder nearby to help you remember what develops. With your eyes either open or comfortably closed, imagine yourself 20 years from today. Where might you be, what might you be doing?

With all the possibilities in the world open to you, imagine what you would most like to do as a career. Imagine what sort of people you would like to associate with, what you might be wearing, how much money you'd like to be earning. Spend most of the time allowing yourself to imagine any and all avenues your imagery might take. Make note of each and every idea, description, and possibility that comes up, no matter how absurd or unlikely.

Now imagine all the obstacles that might keep you from achieving *any* imagined future you have just described for yourself. Would you not be able to enjoy one of those careers because of a lack of education, bad economic conditions, government regulations, your spouse, your appearance, your age, your family, lack of capital, or any other reason?

Finally, imagine how you might overcome each of the obstacles you have described. How might you use your talent, resources, and abilities, both present and future, to counteract the negative forces inhibiting you from any of your imagined careers? This exercise is a form of brainstorming with yourself. In this instance, the only person who can help you set goals for yourself is you. When you use a relaxed state of imagery you are also using your unconscious to uncover the desires you may not consciously be aware of.

Often we deny a possibility to ourselves for reasons known only to the unconscious. The best way to dissolve those blockages is to go to the unconscious and allow such cloaked desires to percolate up to the conscious in the form of imagined goals. This exercise will stimulate just such a process. However, you may need to practice it several times before you have enough material to select a basic set of goals that you are excited about.

Excitement and enthusiasm are precisely the emotional feelings that make objectives dynamic and meaningful in our lives. If we cannot get excited about our goals, a lack of motivation will often prevent us from taking the necessary action to accomplish them. The test of whether a goal or objective is right for you is how excited you are about it. The excitement is best when it can be sustained. Look for the sort of enthusiasm that lasts; in other words, if you look at those written goals a week later, are you still as enthused as you were originally?

REACHING YOUR DESTINATION

The second aspect of goal setting is to mentally rehearse how you will achieve each of your objectives. Once you have established the objectives you wish to reach, short-term, intermediate, and long-range, you can begin to formulate the specific tactics to put them in your grasp. Here is what we mean: Daniel is the manager of a marketing division. He created the following set of effective goals, supported by the A.I.M. Plan.

Long-range goal, 3–5 years: "Live in the 5-bedroom home I walked through with my wife several weeks ago. I can create a mental image of that house easily in my mind, the colors, the flowers blooming outside, the aromas of the different parts of the house, the sounds of the birds and the occasional passing car. The home I will be living in has a small lake and a corral for two horses."

Short-range goal, 2 years: "I will be promoted to the position of vice president of marketing with an annual salary of $55,000 plus the benefit package worth $10,000. I will have two secretaries, an office with a view of the open city, and access to the company jet."

One-year goal: "Implement the vertical integration of the new product line and show a 15 percent ($750,000) increase in sales volume for the base product line."

Tactical goals: "First, immediately begin a payroll deduction of 8 percent of my monthly salary to be invested in a growth-oriented mutual fund recommended by my financial planner to serve as a down payment for the new house.

"Next, select the most capable person on my team to head a task force to bring to market the new product line and have the task force in action within 30 days."

You can quickly see that Daniel has deliberated and detailed his goals in a progressive and interrelated manner. We have not reprinted his entire set of tactical goals because space was limited, but his tactical goals numbered 27 and went into very specific detail related to his work.

In the imagery Daniel creates from these tactical, short-range, and long-term goals, he sees the colors, feels the textures, smells the aromas, tastes the wine, and hears the sounds involved. It is that total involvement of many of the senses simultaneously that registers most indelibly on the unconscious mind.

If it seems we have placed a great deal of emphasis on setting effective goals, it is because without them the A.I.M. program is aimed at nothing. Well designed goals that you are excited about are like magnets. They pull people, events, your concentration, and action in the direction of their achievement.

Time Competence

Earlier we provided some techniques for improving your time management; triage of your daily, weekly, and monthly activities, and maintaining a bias for action. An imagery tactic for using your most productive time in an efficient manner is to mentally rehearse predictable activities beforehand.

You can begin with the 80/20 rule of productivity we mentioned earlier. That is, most people accomplish 80 percent of their productivity in 20 percent of available work time, and vice versa. In a brief 15-minute exercise you can compress your day and mentally rehearse how you would prioritize your daily activities. One technique is to imagine an "80" box and a "20" box. You can toss all the tasks, obligations, and activities in your day into either.

However, in your imagery you can alter which tasks go into which box. If more are going into the 20 percent box, you are planting the notion in your unconscious that you will prefer actions that link with productivity rather than nonactivity or busywork.

Another tactic is to use your mental rehearsal speed-up or slow-down time references and your perception of time passing. Have you ever noticed that time seems to pass more quickly when you are doing something enjoyable, yet it moves as slow as sap when you are bored? If it were not for the markers of time in our lives, we would not be accurately aware of the passage of time. This has been demonstrated in experiments where individuals have been deprived of normal indicators of time passing, such as clocks, daylight and night, regular food intervals, and sleeping patterns.

Your imagery can compress or expand the amount of time required to perform specific activities. For example, if you know that you will be conducting a particular meeting that often runs longer than scheduled, mentally rehearse how you will handle the meeting to stay on schedule. First, slow the meeting down in your imagery to observe certain individuals, processes, or procedures more closely, looking for the time-consuming element.

Then, speed the activity up and streamline your actions to be more efficient. If for example, you noticed that two particular topics of the meeting required more discussion than others, imagine what would happen if you planned to deal with them combined or consecutively to minimize unneeded discussion time.

Implicit in your mental rehearsals is the bias for action, which hyper-performers possess. As you mentally replay the sequences of events, look for opportunities to act instead of postpone. A big time-eater in some large organizations is the fear or inhibition to act. If you rehearse the 80 percent of your day, which produces only 20 percent of productivity, with the goal of taking action whenever possible, you will increase your time efficiency and productivity measurably.

Building Toward Greater Success

As you may have noticed, many of the tactics for one trait can be applied to others. You will quickly find that your imagery and mental rehearsal exercises will have a positive ripple effect on many other aspects of your daily performance beyond the specifics you are working on. The cumulative effects of these mental processes combined with active relaxation will produce a reinforcement of the exercises themselves.

In the next chapter we will discuss various ways in which you can incorporate the A.I.M. Superskills into your daily life, or into your organization.

7

Putting It All Together

*T*here is a great amount of individuality in using active relaxation. Each person is likely to have slightly different needs and varying levels of stress and tension to release. You will certainly find that some days require more relaxation time than other days, just to reach the same level of calm.

If you are new to active relaxation, set aside time for two 15-minute exercises, once in the morning, and again at midday before lunch, right before dinner, or in early evening. In the beginning it is best to set aside separate time for active relaxation and imagery because the most important element, initially, is to allow yourself to fully relax.

After you have experienced active relaxation and can relax easily and quickly, you can then combine the relaxation exercise with imagery by first spending about five minutes exclusively relaxing your body, using a brief version of active relaxation described in Chapter 4.

Be certain that you take the time necessary to develop a relaxed body and mind before your imagery exercises, because you will find a much richer experience, and you will produce faster results with your imagery. Also, we have found that it is more effective to work on one or two goals at a time. One tactic is to work on one goal exclusively in your relaxed imagery and mental rehearsals the first week. Then on the second week begin to also develop imagery of a second goal, and in the third week imagery for the new goal only. On the fourth week the cycle repeats with the introduction of a new goal.

While this will produce rapid and noticeable changes, we have also realized that after some practice, a great many of our seminar attendees regularly work on several objectives simultaneously and have quite satisfactory results. However, we recommend that you begin the A.I.M. program by selecting what you feel are the most important two or three goals to work on first.

You may want to develop traits that most directly relate to projects or activities you are currently involved in, or specific traits you have found you are weak in, in the Personal Inventory Profile. As to how much time to devote to mental rehearsal and imagery, we suggest 15 to 20 minutes per day, not necessarily all at once. But in most cases we have found that imagery produces results even if practiced for very brief periods of time. In short, any imagery is much better than none at all. So, naturally, scheduling some space in your daily routine for five minutes of quiet time to image your objectives and goals is certainly going to produce noticeable results in a short time.

When you have gained some proficiency in developing imagery, you will find that you can close your eyes for a few moments just about anywhere and begin imagining clearly even in the midst of noise and crowds. We have seen many people in an airport waiting to board use the time for a few minutes of imagery. When you have developed a specific plan for using mental rehearsal and imagery and you are repeating specific imagery sequences for reinforcement, it will be easy to take several deep breaths, close your eyes, and reinstitute a mental picture you are familiar with.

Time Required to See Results

Many influences are particular to the individual using the relaxation and imagery techniques, and therefore there is a broad range of result patterns possible. In some cases you may see results almost immediately. For example, present centering can produce a noticeable change within a day, while a goal of increased time efficiency may require more practice until you see a tangible difference.

If you are working on reversing changes in habits or behavior patterns that you have had for many years you may need to work on those changes more intently to effect noticeable progress. A difference will be apparent more quickly in areas where you already have momentum.

How to Use the A.I.M. Program
Within an Organization

First, to increase the productivity, spirit, and cohesiveness of your team, you need to have the players you can develop these qualities in and then instill them with the vision of what the team is trying to accomplish. Then the A.I.M. program on an individual basis will encourage each to achieve their individual best. Many corporations and organizations may find it awkward to conduct group imagery sessions. However, the evidence is very clear that group practice is even more powerful than individual work.

In a workshop environment, group practice of active relaxation, imagery, and mental rehearsal develops the team spirit and encourages the participants to help and encourage each other. Often knowledgeable outside specialists can conduct the workshop and then teach motivated company individuals to be team leaders who can then conduct workshops on the A.I.M. program for new employees and ongoing reinforcement workshops. Team leaders can use imagery suggestions in their presentations, and encourage employees and help them use imagery for work-related issues.

How Management Can Use the Program

First, identify what types of players are on your management team. The Personal Inventory Profile in this book will help determine where individuals are as related to optimal performance. An independent consulting group or a staff psychologist can also assist in this area. The main objective here is to determine who on the team are Type A and Type B SOPs, who are classic Type B personalities, and who are new workaholics. A CEO can review subordinates to see how consistently productive the individuals are, how healthy they have been, and whether they appear happy or unhappy in their work.

The new workaholics will usually stand out as the team stars, the obvious achievers. The stressed-out people will make up the bulk of the team and the classic Type B managers will often be the ones that the CEO has difficulty relating to.

The next thing you must do if you have new workaholic individuals working for you is develop ways to keep them. Here are steps you can take to do this:

1. Be certain that the individual is not an SOP.

2. Provide responsibility and autonomy. New workaholics need both of these in order to have control and challenge. These, of course, are associated with accountability. If new workaholics are not given responsibility and autonomy they will soon leave for a position that does provide these elements.

3. They must have feedback. Everyone needs feedback, but new workaholics are especially sensitive to it. They need feedback for two reasons: first, as a yardstick to measure themselves by; second, like all of us, they need positive strokes. New workaholics want to know how well they are doing and how what they are doing fits into the company plans. This feedback can come in many forms: one-on-one praise, acknowledgment in groups, such as awards, presentations, and perhaps in company newsletters or other public notices, and certainly in promotions, raises, or bonuses. Though new workaholics are not primarily motivated by money, compensation is important and should not be overlooked as part of the feedback process. In most work environments money is still regarded as the sincerest form of flattery. However, verbal rewards are often just as important as more tangible ones.

Questions and Answers

We have compiled a series of frequently asked questions about the A.I.M. program, and offer them here, as they may answer questions you may have also.

Q. What if I fall asleep when I'm doing my active relaxation?

A. Active relaxation involves your conscious and unconscious mind, so that falling asleep will not be so frequent a problem as you might think. If it does happen, it may be that you really needed the sleep. However, if you are falling asleep during the relaxation exercise, these are some changes you can make to prevent that from happening:

1. Change your position.
2. Change the time of day you do the relaxation.
3. Speed up the relaxation process a bit.

Q. What do I do if I can't visualize?

A. We all image as we perceive the world; we can image in the five senses. Those people who do not use visual imagery do use feeling imagery or hearing imagery very well. Also, almost everyone uses the visual sense of an event, action, person, or place even if it is not a vivid picture, more like seeing with the mind's eye. For example, answer the question: How many windows do you have in your home or apartment? In order to answer that question you must mentally count the windows even if you don't mentally picture the walls and rooms. That is using your mind's eye, a visual sense of the place without the actual picture. In the same way, each of us has a mind's ear that provides an impression of sound even in the absence of the mental recreation of the sound.

The most important aspect of imagery is that you control the images, without necessarily having the images vivid. In fact, overly vivid imaging can be a drawback because there is a tendency to focus too closely on the images and not enough on making the images do what you desire them to do.

Q. How can I improve my ability to image?

A. First, most people believe that to image means to visualize, and as we said earlier, imaging can be done with any of the five senses, not merely visually. Beyond pointing that out, we would suggest that practicing imagery is the best way to improve. We do not believe that specific work on improving your imaging abilities is necessary. We have experimented with a host of techniques—sleep deprivation, isolation tanks, flashing colored lights—and none have delivered any significant changes.

The immediate sensory gratification from imaging is not what produces long-term results. Rather than trying to improve imaging techniques, it is more important to improve the control and direction of your imaging experiences. As we have said before, the only thing you can really do wrong in your imagery is not to do it.

Q. As head of a large organization, how can I help my managers improve their optimal performance traits?

A. You must first evaluate whether or not they wish to be helped. You cannot make someone into an optimal performer; you can only help someone reach that objective if he or she is self-motivated to do so. Books such as this are one way to learn new workaholic skills. Seminars and workshops that focus on developing or improving high-level achievement are another source of assistance. Another way to indirectly help others is to make helpful information and materials available to them. Circulate relevant newspaper articles, magazine pieces, and books, keep brochures and other items of interest in your office. When the seed begins to germinate you will notice an individual may ask you a question about one of the items you have made available.

Q. What if the people in my organization don't want to change?

A. If people in your organization refuse help or have no desire to work toward optimal performance, then you can't do anything to help them, but you can help yourself. First, you can learn more about improving your own specific weak areas and second, you can be an example to the others in your organization. Often the only way to motivate others is for them to see an example of what a program or technique will do when practiced for a given period of time. In this subtle way, as a role model or mentor, you may be able to influence borderline SOPs to use some new skills to gain even more skill.

Q. Which is more effective, end-result imagery or mental rehearsal imagery?

A. Though both are effective and of essential value to creating self-directed change, we have found end-result imagery to be the most effective and the more universally applicable. If you are presented with a situation where mental rehearsal is difficult because the process may be too complicated, end-result imagery will be more than sufficient to create improvement. And incidentally, if you do have a complex or lengthy process for mental rehearsal you may be able to segment the actions and rehearse them as components.

Q. What if I don't want to be a new workaholic, a hyperperformer, an old workaholic, or any kind of workaholic?

A. To begin, we want to avoid getting lost in a semantic jungle of terms, yet it is important to understand what the various concepts refer to in the workplace so that you can decide what you want to be and what you don't want to be. It is not the intention of this book to propose that being a new workaholic is intrinsically better than not being one. However, it is clear from the research and studies that have been done that those individuals we call new workaholics are among the healthiest and most productive members of our society.

If you are happy being a classic Type B then we heartily suggest you not try to change. In fact, for a classic Type B to try to become a new workaholic may bring about more stress than is healthy. However, if you are unhappy being a classic Type A, or what we call a stressed-out person, and want to improve your performance to your fullest potential, then the techniques in this book are valuable for you. Alternatively, if you feel you are closer to being a classic Type B personality, then you may wish to develop those traits. After all, classic Type Bs are not illness prone.

We have pointed out the vast difference between previous concepts of workaholism, represented by SOPs, and the new workaholism, represented by high-level achievers. If it is the term workaholic or new workaholic that troubles you and you have a difficult time relating to the terms, use synonyms such as healthy Type A behavior, or high-level achiever, or hearty, happy worker. We are not championing the labels, but we are presenting a practical method of increasing one's performance level. It is up to the individual to decide whether or not increased performance levels are worthwhile objectives to pursue.

Q. Isn't workaholism or new workaholism an addiction?

A. You can say that both old and new workaholism are addictions to work. However, old workaholism is a negative addiction and new workaholism is a positive addiction. William Glasser, author of *Positive Addiction,* talks about exercise and meditation, and feels that the old notion of workaholism is a negative addiction, like alcoholism. Further, the concept of addiction suggests a dependency upon something that, if removed, will cause clinical, physical symptoms— generally speaking, harmful, unwanted symptoms.

A positive addiction is not harmful, but actually beneficial, and therefore not really an addiction at all in the clinical sense.

On the other hand, if you are an SOP and a workaholic in the old sense of the word, then you will be suffering negative symptoms of stress and, indeed, you may be suffering from addiction.

Some Final Comments

What we have presented is a program for developing your personal best in business and personal endeavors. The individuals we have worked with in private counseling, in-service workshops, seminars, and in consultation with other health-care professionals, have verified that the A.I.M. Superskills that have been proven to create hyper-performance in athletes do have the same positive results in business applications.

In a period of change in both the role of work in our society and the competitiveness within the workplace, these skills will make a dramatic positive change for motivated individuals willing to implement them in a regular and ongoing program. The value of hyper-performance can be most easily seen in the rewards of being a high-level achiever. Look within your organization, your industry, or your community and those achievers will stand out.

The payoff is not just recognition and financial gain. More importantly, it is a sense of personal gratification of accomplishment and personal worth, which provide you with a radiant feeling of self-confidence in the knowledge that virtually anything you develop as a priority can be achieved.

We always conclude our workshops and seminars with an invitation to participants to provide feedback on how these Superskills have effected change in their lives. We invite readers of this book to let us know of their experiences. Write to us in care of Pratt/Korn & Associates, Inc., Scripps Hospital Medical Building, 9834 Genessee Avenue, Suite 321, La Jolla, California, 92037, or in care of the publisher.

References

Abodaher, D. *Iacocca*. New York: Macmillan, 1982.

Ahsen, A. "Eidetics: An overview." *Journal of Mental Imagery* (1977).

Alman, B.M., and Lambrou, P.T. *Self-Hypnosis: A Complete Manual for Health and Self-Change*. San Diego: International Health Publications, 1983.

Anthony, W.P., Wheatley, W., and Maddox, N. "Better Management Through the Mind's Eye." *American Management Magazine*, Nov. 1985.

Bach, R. *Illusions*. New York: Delacorte Press/Eleanor Friede, 1977.

Bartolome, F., and Evans, P.A.L. "Must Success Cost So Much?" *Harvard Business Review*, March/April 1980.

Begg, I., Upfold, D., and Wilton, T.D. "Imagery and Verbal Communication." *Journal of Mental Imagery* (1978).

Benson, H. *The Mind / Body Effect*. New York: Simon & Schuster, 1979.

————. *The Relaxation Response*. New York: Avon Books, 1976.

Blanchard, K. and Johnson, S. *The One Minute Manager*. New York: William Morrow, 1982.

Burns, D.D. *Feeling Good: The New Mood Therapy*. New York: William Morrow, 1980.

Cohen, H. *You Can Negotiate Anything*. Secaucus, New Jersey: Stuart, 1980.

Cox, A. *Making of the Achiever*. New York: Dodd, Mead, 1985.

Cousins, N. *Anatomy of an Illness*. New York: W. W. Norton, 1980.

————. *The Healing Heart*. New York: W. W. Norton, 1983.

Csikszentmihalyi, M. "Play and Intrinsic Rewards." *Journal of Humanistic Psychology* 15(1975).

Downey, C. "American Way." Report on on-going Purdue University study by Prof. William Theobald, Feb. 5, 1985.

Frankl, V. *Man's Search for Meaning*, Rev. ed. New York: Washington Square Press, 1984.

Friedman, H.S., Hall, J.A., and Harris, M.J. "Type A Behavior, Nonverbal Expressive Style, and Health." *Journal of Personality and Social Psychology* 48(1985).

Friedman, M., and Rosenman, R.H. *Type A Behavior and Your Heart.* New York: Fawcett, 1974.

Gallway, T. *The Inner Game of Tennis.* New York: Random House, 1974.

_____, and Kreigel, B. *Inner Skiing.* New York: Random House, 1977.

Garfield, C.A. *Peak Performers: The New Heroes of American Business.* New York: William Morrow, 1986.

_____. *Peak Performance.* New York: Tarcher, 1984.

_____. "How to Achieve Peak Performance." Paper presented at a workshop on "Peak Performance" San Francisco, May 1981.

Girdan, D.A., and Everly, G.S. *Controlling Stress and Tension.* Englewood Cliffs, NJ: Prentice Hall, 1986.

Gschwandtner, G. *Superachievers: Portraits of Success.* Englewood Cliffs, NJ: Prentice Hall, 1984.

Holt, P.R. "On the Nature of Generality and Mental Imagery." In P.W. Sheehan (Ed.), *The Nature and Function of Imagery.* New York: Academic, 1972.

Horowitz, M.J. "Image Formation: Clinical Observations of Cognitive Model." In P.W. Sheehan (Ed.), *The Nature and Function of Imagery.* New York: Academic, 1972.

_____. "Visual Imagery and Cognitive Organization." *American Journal of Psychiatry* (1967).

Jacobson, E. *Anxiety and Tension Control.* New York: J.B. Lippincott, 1964.

_____. *Progressive Relaxation.* Chicago: University of Chicago Press, 1942.

_____. "Electrical Measurements of Neuromuscular States During Mental Activities;" "(IV) Evidence of Contraction of Specific Muscles During Imagination;" "(V) Variation of Specific Muscles Contracting During Imagination." *American Journal of Physiology* 96(1931): 115–21.

Kobasa, S.C., and Maddi, S.R. *The Hardy Executive: Health Under Stress.* Homewood, IL: Dow Jones-Irwin, 1984.

Kobasa, S.C. "How Much Stress Can You Survive." *American Health,* Sept. 1984.

_____. "Stressful Life Events, Personality & Health: An Inquiry Into Hardiness." *Journal of Personality and Social Psychology* 37(1979).

Kolanay, B. "The Effects of Visual Motor Behavior Rehearsal on Athletic Performance." Unpublished master's thesis, Hunter College, City University of New York, 1977.

Korn, E.R., and Pratt, G.J. "Workaholism: The Sign of Success." *The Hospital Manager,* Jan. 1986.

Korn, E.R., and Johnson, K. *Visualization: The Uses of Imagery in the Health Professions.* Homewood, IL: Dow Jones-Irwin, 1983.

Lakein, A. *How to Get Control of Your Time and Your Life.* New York: Peter A. Wyden, 1973.

Leavitt, H.J. *Corporate Pathfinders.* Homewood, IL: Dow Jones-Irwin, 1986.

Leonard, G. *The Ultimate Athlete.* New York: Viking Press, 1975.

Locke, S.E. "Stress, Adaptation and Immunity: Studies in Humans." *General Hospital Psychiatry,* March 1982.

Machlowitz, M. *Workaholics: Living With Them, Working With Them.* Reading, MA: Addison-Wesley, 1980.

Maltz, M. *Psycho-Cybernetics.* New York: Pocket Books, 1966.

Maslow, A. *Religions, Values and Peak-Experiences.* New York: Viking, 1964.

Morse, D.R., and Furst, M.L. *Women Under Stress.* New York: Van Nostrand Reinhold, 1982.

Murphy, M. *Golf in the Kingdom.* New York: Viking Press, 1972.

Nicklaus, J. *Golf My Way.* New York: Simon & Schuster, 1974.

Palmore, E. *Social Patterns in Normal Aging: Findings From the Duke University Longitudinal Study.* Durham, NC: Duke University Press, 1981.

Pascarella, P. *The New Achievers: Creating a Modern Work Ethic.* New York: Free Press, 1984.

Pearce, J.C. *The Crack in the Cosmic Egg.* New York: Washington Square Press, 1971.

Pelletier, K. *Mind as Healer/Mind as Slayer.* New York: Dell, 1977.

————. *Healthy People in Unhealthy Places.* New York: Delta Press, 1984.

Peters, R.K., Benson, H., and Porter, D. "Daily Relaxation Response Breaks in a Working Population: Effects on Self-Reported Measures of Health, Performance, and Well-Being." *American Journal of Public Health* 67(1977).

Pratt, G.J., Wood, D.P., and Alman, B.M. *A Clinical Hypnosis Primer.* La Jolla, CA: Psychology & Consulting Associates Press, 1984.

Pribram, K.H. "What the Fuss Is All About." *Re-Vision* 1(1978).

Privette, G. "Experience as a Component of Personality Theory." *Psychological Reports* (1985).

Quick, J.C., and Quick, J.D. *Organizational Stress and Preventative Management.* New York: McGraw-Hill, 1984.

Richardson, A. *Mental Imagery.* New York: Springer, 1969.

Samuels, M., and Samuels, N. *Seeing With the Mind's Eye.* New York: Random House, 1975.

Selye, H. *The Stress of Life,* 2d rev. ed. New York: McGraw-Hill. 1978.

Silver, A.D. *Entrepreneurial Megabucks.* New York: Wiley, 1985.

Veninga, R.L., and Spradley, J.P. *The Work Stress Connection.* Boston: Little, Brown, 1981.

Waitley, D. *Seeds of Greatness.* Old Tappan, NJ: Revell, 1983.

Williams, R.B., et. al. "Type A Behavior, Hostility, and Coronary Atherosclerosis." *Journal of Psychosomatic Medicine* 42(1980).

Index

Absenteeism, 25, 97
Active relaxation, 9, 23, 27, 54, 66,
    70, 72, 74, 75, 87, 89, 98–104,
    127–148, 177, 183
Adams, A., 5
Adaptability, 9, 31, 36, 69, 140, 151,
    152
Addition, 25, 26, 82, 186, 187
Adrenalin, 21
A.I.M., 9, 27, 28, 54, 66, 75, 84, 88,
    89, 99, 104, 107, 116, 145,
    148, 170, 173, 178, 183, 188
  benefits of, 117
  within an organization, 180
Anderson, R., 131
Anthony, W.P., 120, 121, 129
Anxiety, 15, 22, 89, 93, 116
Aristotle, 112
Arthritis, 22
Asimov, I., 10

Bach, R., 37, 45
Bartolome, F., 71
Beck, A., 152, 159
Beethoven, L., 49, 65
Ben-Gurion, D., 8
Benson, H., 95, 96, 98, 99
Biochemical response, 21
Bioelectrical responses, 107, 112. *See
    also* Engrams
Bio-feedback, 19, 97
Brainstorming, 67, 87, 156, 169
Breathing, 15, 72, 93, 95–104, 160

Burnout, 5, 6, 19
Burns, G., 131

Cancer, 22
Career, 14, 33, 58, 168
Cartland, B., 131
Cathcart, J., 11
Charbonneau, J., 120
Cholesterol, 77, 78, 96
Cocaine, 7
Cognitive strategy, 69, 152
Cognitive Theory of Depression (Beck), 159
Cohen, H., 43
Comfort zone, 36–38
Control, 10, 15–17, 67, 78, 86–89,
    100, 132, 148, 184
  critical element of, 14
  lack of, 4, 79
  and personal power, 43, 44
  as unconscious valve, 111, 112, 165
Corporate Pathfinders (Leavitt), 165
Cousins, N., 96
Cox, A., 50, 57
The Crack in the Cosmic Egg (Pearce),
    164
Creativity, 4, 9, 31, 52, 53, 69, 86,
    113, 129, 140, 150, 164–166
Csikszentmihaly, M., 85
Cues, 155

Daydreaming, 117
Decision-making, 37, 60, 130
Depression, 16, 23, 25, 120